Published by Pedigree in association with **Yours**
Pedigree Books Limited, Beech Hill House, Walnut Gardens, Exeter, Devon EX4 4DH

Yours – the leading magazine for women over 50. Look out for it in your local newsagent.
Yours – Bretton Court, Bretton, Peterborough PE3 8DZ. Tel: 01733 264666

Your Health: Please consult your doctor if you are unsure about taking any medication recommended in our health section, especially if you are already on medication.

Compiled and edited by Caroline Chadderton
Designed by David Reid
Sub-edited by Christine Curtis
Additional writing by Charlotte Haigh, Gareth Salter, Marion Clark,
Katy Lamb, Sharon Reid and Paul Whenman
With thanks to the following for recipes and picures: Quality Standard Beef, Fruisana,
The Fresh Cut Stir Fry Alliance, Billington's, Tate & Lyle, British Trout Association, British Asparagus,
The Dairy Council, The Vegetarian Society

*And special thanks to all the readers who have contributed so wonderfully to this Year Book
by sending in their memories, photographs, stories and tips*

£6.99

Back in January 2006, while you were just starting to enjoy last year's Year Book, Associate Ed, Caroline, was worrying about this one. It's the same every year, Caroline is sure we can never produce another Year Book that can possibly top the last one. How could you, the readers, possibly come up with better stories, tips and memories than the year before? By April/May she is starting to look a bit happier as she works through the huge pile of letters you've sent in. And as the year progresses, gradually she has that 'look' that says, yes – it could just be, once again, the best Year Book we have ever produced.

So a huge thank you to all the contributors, plus our talented design and subbing team for putting it all together. But chiefly to you – the letter-writers of **Yours** – for once again putting a smile on Caroline's face.

Valery

Valery McConnell
Editor, **Yours**

There's no doubting that you've excelled yourselves with this Year Book, not only with your lovely stories, poems and photographs, but by the sheer number that flooded into the office. By March last year, I was surrounded by hundreds of letters taking up most of my desk and overflowing onto the floor. That was before I started smiling…

What a privilege to read all of them – your Dads, your special songs, your diary entries – you made me laugh out loud, gave me pause for thought and I confess I reached for the tissues more than once.

I hope you try the recipes, enjoy growing some herbs this year and find the tips useful.

I'm sorry that we couldn't include everyone's stories, and to those of you who didn't make the Year Book, thank you for sharing your memories with us.

Enjoy your Year Book during 2007.

Caroline

Caroline Chadderton
Associate Editor (Features), **Yours**

January 2007

Monday
1
New Year's Day (Bank Holiday)

Tuesday
2
Bank Holiday (Scotland)

Wednesday
3

Thursday
4

Friday
5

Saturday
6
Epiphany

Sunday
7

Monday
8

Tuesday
9

Wednesday
10

Thursday
11

Friday
12

Saturday
13

Sunday
14

Monday
15

Tuesday
16

Wednesday
17

Thursday
18

Friday
19

Saturday
20

Sunday
21

Monday
22

Tuesday	Sunday
23	**28**
Wednesday	Monday
24	**29**
Thursday	Tuesday
25	**30**
Robert Burns' Night	
Friday	Wednesday
26	**31**
Saturday	
27	
Holocaust Memorial Day	

Praying for snow

"Oh, where is the snow?" the children cry,
"When will the world be white?"
Morn after morn, a despondent sigh;
They'd prayed it would snow in the night.

Sullen, the grey skies threaten and glower,
Pavements, all rain-washed, shine.
Suddenly, sunshine for an hour,
Then the cruel wind's shrill whine.

Round and about the grown-ups walk;
Gone is their Christmas glow.
Of sales, now, and cheap summer hols, they talk,
But the children still wait for the snow.

Mrs Alma Olive, Epsom, Surrey

PIC: J.DAVID ANDREWS/MASTERFILE

My Dad

For years my late Dad, Sam, was a bus driver in North London. On his early shift he usually picked up an old man during the route. One day the old man wasn't there, but my father had noticed him running up a side street to try and catch the bus.

Dad immediately put the bus into reverse and backed right up to the corner to pick up his elderly passenger. An Inspector who witnessed this, reported it to the Bus Station Manager, and my father was commended for his thoughtfulness and consideration.

Shortly after this, Cadbury's were running a campaign to award their CDM medal for worthy actions. I wrote to them about father's kindness and he was duly awarded the CDM. The bonus was that both he and I received a large block of Cadbury's Dairy Milk – I still have his CDM, but the chocolate didn't last long!

Patricia Hines, Eaton Socon, Cambs

Above: Patricia's father, Sam flanked by his CDM memorabilia

Top Tip

Write in your address book in pencil to make it easier to change addresses.
Charlotte Joseph, Lelant

Your January health

Did you know sugar can depress your immune system for up to five hours after eating it? That could leave you vulnerable to bugs, so satisfy your sweet tooth with dried or fresh fruit instead, and try sprinkling cereals and porridge with sweet spices like cinnamon and nutmeg rather than sugar. Your post-Christmas waistline will thank you too!

Meet my pet

Monkshill Jupiter is a nine-month-old Shetland pony – but he answers to Roo. Every morning he's given a make-over by his owners Andrea and Rachael; all the mud is brushed off until his chestnut coat is glossy and his tail sleek. And it's a full-time job as there's nothing he likes better than a roll in the mud!

As he's still only young, he's being trained on his lead rope and he has two other horses in the field to play with.
Andrea Martin, Rochester, Kent

Roo (left) with his half-brother, Florio

Healthy herbs

What is a herb?

This may seem a simple question, but there are several different answers depending on whether you're a botanist, naturalist or gardener. The easiest definition identifies a herb as a plant whose stems, leaves or flowers are used in cooking, medicinally or around the home. If you haven't grown herbs, or have limited yourself to just a few of the more common ones, then experiment this year – the natural world, and plants especially, have a great deal to offer us all.

Top of the hit parade!

7 Jan 1955:
Dickie Valentine
Finger Of Suspicion

4 Jan 1957:
Guy Mitchell
Singing The Blues

3 Jan 1963:
Cliff Richard
The Next Time / Bachelor Boy

Recipe of the week

Beef Supper in a Flash
(Serves 2)

- 15 ml (1 tablespoon) sunflower oil
- 25 g (1 oz) plain flour mixed with 5 ml (1 tsp) paprika powder
- Salt and freshly milled black pepper
- 225 g (8 oz) lean rump or sirloin steaks, cut into 10 cm (4 inch) strips
- 1 red onion, peeled and sliced
- 2 cloves garlic, peeled and finely chopped
- 175 g (6 oz) new potatoes, cooked and halved
- Dash Worcestershire sauce
- 300 ml (½ pint) good, hot beef stock
- 100 g (4 oz) cherry tomatoes, halved
- 15 ml (1 tablespoon) freshly chopped parsley or chives

1 Heat the oil in a large frying pan.
2 Meanwhile, place the flour in a large bowl or plastic bag and mix together with the paprika and seasoning. Toss the beef strips in the flour.
3 Cook the beef for 3-4 minutes, stirring occasionally. Add the onion, garlic and potatoes and cook for a further 2-3 minutes.
4 Add the Worcestershire sauce, seasoning (if required), stock and cherry tomatoes and heat for 1-2 minutes.
5 Sprinkle over the parsley or chives.
6 Serve immediately with seasonal vegetables and garlic bread.

RECIPE COURTESY QUALITY STANDARD BEEF

Well I never...

'The Americans may have need of the telephone but we do not. We have plenty of messenger boys'

Sir William Preece, chief engineer of the General Post Office in Britain (1876).

Well I never…

'Cleaning your house while your kids are still growing is like shovelling the walk before it stops snowing'.

Phyllis Diller

Recipe of the week

Oat Cookies with Raisins

(Makes 25)

- 125 g (5 oz) margarine
- 125 g (5 oz) Fruisana Fruit Sugar
- 50 g (2 oz) raisins
- 125 g (5 oz) wholemeal flour
- 250 g (10 oz) oat flakes
- 5 ml (1 teaspoon) baking powder
- 5 ml (1 teaspoon) mixed spice
- 60 ml (4 tablespoons) skimmed milk

1 Preheat the oven to 200°C, 400°F, or Gas Mark 6.
2 Cream the margarine and the Fruisana Fruit Sugar together until pale.
3 Chop the raisins into small pieces. Sieve together all of the dry ingredients and add to the creamed mixture, followed by the raisins.
4 Add the milk gradually and mix thoroughly.
5 Mould spoonfuls of the mixture into round shapes and place in paper cases. Flatten slightly with the back of a spoon.
6 Bake at 200°C, 400°F, or Gas Mark 6 in the centre of the oven for 20 minutes.

RECIPE COURTESY FRUISANA

Healthy herbs

How can I grow herbs?

There are hundreds of different herbs – just look in your garden centre these days and you'll be amazed at the range – so you can be sure that you'll find plenty that suit your garden, however large or small it may be. Even if you only have a few containers, or perhaps just a windowsill, there are an almost limitless number of herbs you can try. There's nothing better than adding a few fresh leaves straight from the garden to spice up your food – healthy, natural and completely free. And no artificial colouring, flavourings or additives.

Top Tip

Tie a coloured ribbon to your suit case handle to see it on an airport carousel.

Jan Savage, Ipswich

Top of the hit parade!

Janet and her mum and dad working up an appetite for tea

My Dad

My fondest memory of my Dad is our walks on Sunday afternoons. After a big Sunday lunch we would wash up, sit down with a nice cup of tea, and wait for Dad to say: "Coming for a walk, then?" I would groan to myself, 'Oh no, not another walk'.

Off we'd go, dressed in our Sunday best and Dad would walk for miles! I would soon start to get tired and to wonder when we were going home. Footsore and weary, we'd get home just in time for Mum to start getting the tea ready – and were we hungry!

Thinking about those walks, I now realise how lucky I was to be able to walk through all those woods and fields that have now disappeared. The memories of those Sunday afternoon walks with my late Dad are so dear to me now.

Janet Webb, Ashford, Kent

That special song

I was 16 years old in 1960, and had just started courting my husband, whom I had met at a local youth club. That year I was due to take my GCEs and my parents had banned me from going out, because of 'swotting' every night.

We lived in a terraced house which had a small yard and garden with 'backs' running along at the back of the garden, and my bedroom was at the rear, where I'd do my studying.

Most nights Peter, my boyfriend, would walk home along these 'backs' and would whistle the tune To Know Him Is To Love Him by the Teddy Bears. So I used to open my window and wave to him and, sometimes, if the coast was clear, I'd have a romantic conversation with him. (At least I knew he wasn't taking another girl home!)

I went on to pass 7 GCEs, so I suppose it was worth it in the end – and Peter and I have now been married for 40 years!

Marilyn Batho, Stockport

Left: Marilyn as a teenager

Above: Marilyn and Peter

'I shouldn't be here – but I don't care!'

Dear Diary

January 21, 2006

'Hanging 3,000 feet high from a wire, over the Rain Forest in Costa Rica.'

Little did I think that when I answered an advert placed by, my now firm friend, Joy Morgan, in **Yours** seeking a holiday companion to go to South Africa, that I would be in Costa Rica doing this!

What adventures we've had and, hopefully, many more to come, thanks to **Yours**!

Sylvia Higgins, Southport

Top: Sylvia zip-wiring off into the undergrowth!
Above: Sylvia (left) and Joy who became firm friends on holiday

Meet my pet

Our lovely Kitty was born in the garden and has the coat and markings of a Persian cat.

She's full of innovative ideas, such as sunbathing outside in her clean litter tray or perching regularly on top of the magazine rack. And she loves a game of hide and seek.

Kitty knows she's not allowed on the settee but sometimes gets into the lounge to sit in splendour when we have visitors. She's certainly a cat with a sense of humour – have you ever seen a cat laugh? We're sure we have!

Jean Tibbott, Carlisle

Well I never...

The plastic tags on the end of shoelaces are called aglets.

Healthy herbs

Using herbs around the home

Most people are aware that herbs are used in cooking and have, in the past, been used medicinally, but they can also be used around the home. You can use herbs such as lavender, thyme and rosemary in home-made furniture polish, shampoo and cleaners, as well as in air fresheners, insect repellents and drawer liners. They're easy to make and much better than supermarket versions which are usually full of chemicals.

Recipe of the week

Poached Winter Fruits in Vanilla Syrup

- 200 g (7 oz) mixed winter fruits, e.g dates, figs, prunes, cranberries
- 60 ml (4 tablespoons) Light Muscovado sugar
- 1 vanilla pod
- 30 ml (2 tablespoons) white wine

1 Place the fruits in a saucepan; add the sugar, vanilla pod, wine and enough cold water to just cover the fruit.
2 Bring to the boil. Reduce the heat and simmer for several minutes until the fruit is tender. Strain the fruit, reserving the cooking liquid, and set aside.
3 Return the cooking liquid to the heat and cook briskly, reducing the liquid until thick and syrupy. Discard the vanilla pod.
4 Stir the syrup into the fruit and leave to cool.

RECIPE COURTESY BILLINGTON'S

Top Tip

Cut off your name and address from the top of junk mail and stick it on coupons, competitions etc to save time filling them in.
S Morse, Ashby De La Zouch

Top of the hit parade!

16 Jan 1953:
Jo Stafford
You Belong To Me

16 Jan 1964:
Dave Clark Five
Glad All Over

19 Jan 1967:
Monkees
I'm A Believer

My Dad

My Dad, Neville, was a policeman from 1939 to 1963. He achieved Station Sergeant rank and did his time at Richmond, Surrey nick.

He was a figure to fear in uniform – very fair to first offenders but stern to those who re-offended. The kids down our road were told when they misbehaved, 'We'll send for Sergeant Manning,' which scared the pants off them!

Indoors, when the uniform came off, the fun began. Rose, my younger sister, would come into the front room with a jam tart in her hand. Dad would ask what she was holding. Rose would go over and show him the jam tart, which Dad got hold of and squashed in her hand. He caught her every time!

We went on holiday to Wales to stay with his sister, Mizpah,

Ethel's Dad, Station Sergeant Neville Manning, ready for duty

who wasn't a keen cook. So it was decided that Dad and us kids would go to the chippy for faggots and chips. Before that, we'd been putting makeup on him and rolling his hair in pipe cleaners – he was so placid we could do almost anything with him.

So Dad got his coat on and, getting the bowl for the faggots, called us and off we went with him all dolled up – complete with dangly earrings! You should have seen the stares and we caused an uproar in the chippy but Dad didn't turn a (rollered) hair!

Ethel Chance, Shanklin

January 22-28

Recipe of the week

Lemongrass Chicken and Ginger Noodles

(Serves 4)

- ■ 4 chicken breast fillets, sliced into strips
- ■ 15 ml (1 tablespoon) minced lemongrass
- ■ 2 cloves garlic, crushed
- ■ 30 ml (2 tablespoons) sesame oil
- ■ 1 onion, finely sliced
- ■ ½ lemon, finely sliced
- ■ 15 ml (1 tablespoon) grated fresh ginger
- ■ 60 ml (4 tablespoons) hoisin sauce
- ■ 200 ml (7 fl oz) hot water
- ■ 30 ml (2 tablespoons) soy sauce
- ■ 1 x 300 g (approx 11 oz) pack fresh cut egg noodles
- ■ 1 x 300 g (11 oz) pack fresh cut vegetable and beansprout stir- fry
- ■ 3 spring onions, finely shredded

1 Place the chicken in a bowl, add the lemongrass and garlic and mix well, cover and leave to marinate for 30 minutes in the fridge.
2 Heat the wok over a moderate heat. Add the sesame oil and swirl to coat the pan. Stir-fry the chicken for 4-5 minutes, stirring until golden brown and lightly charred around the edges. Transfer to a plate.
3 Increase the heat to high, add the remaining oil, and add the onion, lemon and ginger. Stir-fry for 2 minutes. Add the chicken, hoisin sauce, water and soy sauce and bring to the boil, then simmer for 2 minutes.
4 Finally add the noodles and stir fry vegetables and cook, stirring for a further 1 minute or until the vegetables are just wilted. To serve, tip the chicken noodles into large flat bowls and sprinkle with the spring onions.

RECIPE COURTESY THE FRESH CUT STIR FRY ALLIANCE

Well I never…

'We don't like their sound and guitar music is on the way out'.
Decca Records rejects the Beatles in 1962

Healthy herbs

Herbs in first aid

A large number of herbs can be used to provide simple effective relief for minor injuries and ailments and even disease. It's worth growing a few in the garden and drying their leaves to use in creams, tinctures or ointments, so you can be ready with nature's own antiseptic. On many occasions you can treat the affected area by rubbing it with leaves picked straight from the plant. One example is aloe vera – the juice from its leaves is excellent for treating burns, acne and excema. It thrives in a sunny container – but should be overwintered inside.

My Dad

My special memory of my Dad is the first time I met him, in 2005. My birth was the result of a wartime affair and when I was 10 years old, my mother told me, giving me only his name and the fact that he was a soldier.

All my life I yearned to know what he was like and desperately wanted to find him, but knew it was impossible.

Fifty-one years after being told about him, I decided to look for him through the Old Comrades page in Yours and, unbelievably, I found him!

The first time I met him is indelibly printed on my mind. He stood just inside the door, his stick in one hand and the other stretched out towards me. We hugged, and the tears flowed down my face. I

Cynthia and her dad on their first meeting in 2005

never wanted to let go of him.

We now meet regularly, write and telephone and I think he is the most wonderful person in the world.

Cynthia Brown, Suffolk

That special song

Irene and her husband, Jack

My husband John (always known as Jack) was in the RAF for five years and while in France during the Second World War, had a short leave in France. When he eventually returned home, he said he would take me there one day.

We went in 1960 and how wonderful our time there was. We did all the usual things, visited the Louvre, the Eiffel Tower, had a boat trip on the Seine and went to the Moulin Rouge.

One evening we went to a small restaurant with a dance floor, and orchestra which played Strangers In The Night. We danced on and on; the other dancers left the floor until we were the only couple left. When the music finished, we returned to our table and some of the diners applauded us.

Whenever we heard the tune after that we always remarked, 'They're playing our tune', – what a lovely reminder of our happy time in Paris!

Irene Hacker, Sidcup, Kent

Top Tip

If new school clothes are too stiff and starchy, wash them in salted water and they will come out nice and soft.

Ann O'Halloran, Old Coulsdon

Top of the hit parade!

24 Jan 1958:
Elvis Presley
Jailhouse Rock

24 Jan 1963:
Shadows
Dance On

24 Jan 1968:
Georgie Fame
The Ballad Of Bonnie & Clyde

PIC: THE ZOOLOGICAL SOCIETY OF LONDON (ZSL)

On location at London Zoo

Talk to the animals

If your grandchildren took you along to see all the Harry Potter films, you'll remember that when the dreadful Dursleys took him for a day out at London Zoo our young hero was amazed to discover he could talk to the snakes. But if reptiles give you the creeps, there are plenty of other creatures to choose from – the Zoo has more than 600 species of animals including lions, tigers, primates, giraffes and many more.

Situated in Regent's Park, the Zoo provides the perfect day out at any time of the year. It is the ideal destination for an outing with the grandchildren as there are lots of attractions for youngsters as well as adults. Don't miss the antics of the penguins and pelicans at feeding time. The under-tens will also love meeting farmyard favourites at the 'touch paddock' in the Children's Zoo, where they can stroke or cuddle some of their more domesticated four-legged friends. In the Happy Families area, meerkats are perennially popular, forever up on their hind legs, keeping a watchful eye on the neighbours from their rocky outcrop. Watch the playful otters chasing each other in and out of the pools and waterfalls. The tapirs, too, enjoy a dip in their newly constructed indoor pool. Another recent innovation is an outdoor enclosure where the endangered tamarins can bask in the sunshine.

Older children and grown-ups will learn a lot from a trip around BUGS (which stands for Biodiversity Underpinning Global Survival), an exhibition dedicated to conservation that also explains exactly what is meant by biodiversity. Try not to miss the Animals in Action display, a 30 minute display of animals showing off their amazing flying, foraging and leaping skills.

■ *London Zoo is open every day except Christmas Day. For further information, phone 020 7722 3333 or visit website www.londonzoo.co.uk*

Remember when...
Obadiah, obladee

A one-legged crow visited Barbara Finch of Chapel St Leonards, Lincs

In 1950, aged 16, I was diagnosed with TB and was sent to Scotton Bank Hospital near Knaresborough in Yorkshire. It was very daunting as I had never been away from home before.

There were four of us on our ward which was situated on a veranda, open to the elements. I got terrible chilblains from warming my hands on a tin hot water bottle. The veranda overlooked a grassy field and sometimes a one-legged crow we named Obadiah came up to us for tit-bits.

The sister on our ward was Irish, about five feet tall, and very strict. She would not allow us to run on the ward and, if caught, we were in deep trouble. Because I was the youngest on the ward, I had the unfortunate task of keeping watch when some of the patients went for a smoke.

While I was there, one of the nurses cut my hair. I had ringlets and wanted a more modern style so she cut it short. One of my friends who came to see me said I looked like the film star Joan Fontaine which made me feel good.

After around five months, I was allowed to go out for walks in the countryside, under supervision. When I was sent home, I had to get used to the outside world again. After being in a hospital miles from anywhere the noise of traffic took some getting used to. My small bedroom felt so closed in!

I am now in my 70s and back in hospital, not as a patient but as a volunteer caring for elderly patients. It is a very rewarding job and I love it.

Barbara in 1950, aged 16

The Great British Quiz

Test your knowledge with these fun questions – if you get stuck the answers are at the bottom of the page.

PIC: REX FEATURES

1 At its narrowest point, how wide is the English Channel in miles?
a) 46
b) 21
c) 95
d) 17

2 London was not always the capital of England. Which other city was the nation's capital during the 10th and 11th centuries?
a) Winchester
b) Lincoln
c) Bath
d) York

3 How long is Loch Ness in miles?
a) 32
b) 47
c) 12
d) 23

4 Which composer was responsible for Land of Hope and Glory?
a) William Blake
b) Edward Elgar
c) Henry Purcell
d) Joseph Haydn

5 The river Clyde flows through which Scottish city?
a) Edinburgh
b) Aberdeen
c) Inverness
d) Glasgow

6 What creature is St Patrick said by legend to have banished from Ireland?
a) Snakes
b) Rabbits
c) Foxes
d) Frogs

7 Where is The Prince of Wales invested?
a) Cardiff
b) Cardigan
c) Caernarfon
d) Carephilly

8 The Forth Railway Bridge connects Edinburgh to where?
a) Perth
b) Dundee
c) Dunfermline
d) Fife

9 To the nearest thousand square kilometres what is the land area of Wales?
a) 21,000 square kilometres
b) 46,000 square kilometres
c) 33,000 square kilometres
d) 58,000 square kilometres

10 How high is Mt Snowden?
a) 673 metres
b) 1085 metres
c) 1474 metres
d) 1821 metres

ANSWERS: 1 B, 2 A, 3 D, 4 B, 5 D, 6 A, 7 C, 8 D, 9 A, 10 B

Save the last

Joe hates discos but Anita is determined not to miss a very special party

Anita scooped up the brightly coloured envelope from the doormat and dropped it on the tray with their early morning tea. When she entered the bedroom Joe was still fast asleep. Anita drew back the curtains; her husband spluttered and groaned: "What unearthly time is this, Anita?"

"It's seven o'clock," she answered briskly.

Joe squinted as she waved the envelope under his nose. "Look at this letter!" she told him.

"What about it? I expect it's only another of the January bills."

"Have you ever had a bill arrive in a purple envelope?"

"It's probably a circular of some sort; put it in the bin."

"I think I should open it first."

"Stop twittering and just throw the wretched thing away."

Anita pulled a face. Joe was so crotchety these days. She sighed as she remembered how romantic he used to be.

'Blow him,' she thought, opening the letter. Then she let out a squeal. Joe spilt his tea over the bedclothes and swore.

"We've been invited to a disco!" Anita cried.

Joe's jaw dropped: "A disco? At our age?"

"Isn't it wonderful, Joe?"

"Are you mad? I'd sooner go to my grave than a disco.

Who's it from?"

"Our granddaughter, of course. It's her eighteenth." Anita read out, 'Dear Nana and Pop, I have great pleasure in inviting you both to my special birthday party. It's a disco with eats and it's going to be great. Please, please say you'll come! Love, Megan'.

"We're not going," said Joe, "the music will be deafening, there'll be flashing lights."

"I'll go without you," said Anita, sticking her chin out stubbornly.

"You won't last five minutes with all that noise," Joe told her.

"I'll wear ear muffs."

"And what about the lights?" he asked, "You know you get migraines."

"I'll wear dark glasses."

Joe roared with laughter. "You'll look ridiculous."

Anita put her hand on his arm. "Listen, Joe, Megan is our only grandchild and if she wants us there we must make the effort."

"We could make an excuse."

"No, Joe. For once you must make an effort. This is not about you or me, it's about Megan."

"I'm too old for discos."

"Oh, Joe Edwards! Sometimes I could thump you!"

Half an hour later, when Joe had stomped off down the garden, Anita was on the phone

to her daughter Emma. "Your father won't go," said Anita.

"I knew he'd be difficult, Mum, but Megan wants a photo of all her family together on her eighteenth. Tell him he can leave after that, if he wants to."

When the day came, the local village hall was decked in streamers and balloons. Lights were flashing on and off as someone tested the lasers. Megan and her friends stood in one corner laughing and chattering. Anita helped her daughter set out the food.

Joe hadn't arrived yet and Anita was worried. At the last moment he had agreed to come. They'd had their ups and downs but Joe had always kept his word. She loved him dearly, despite his stubborn ways but she felt, sadly, that his love for her had faded over 40 years of marriage.

An hour later, with the music pounding in her ears, Anita caught sight of him standing in the doorway, looking lost. He glanced around nervously and Anita knew he was ready to turn tail and run. She hurried over and pushed a wad of cotton wool in his hands.

As he stuffed his ears with cotton wool, Megan came across holding hands with a handsome boy: "Hi, Pop, this is Paul! He's been wanting to meet you."

"What?" said Joe.

Megan raised her voice: "I was

"I'd sooner go to my grave than a disco"

dance

by Shelagh Duffy

telling Paul that you used to be quite a mover, Pop, when you and Nana danced to the big bands."

Joe frowned: "It's no use, Megan. I can't hear a word."

Anita took his hand and led him to the adjoining room. "We'll help Emma with the food, dear. It's quieter in there."

"What a spread," said Joe, rubbing his hands together, "When do we eat?"

"Later, Dad," said Emma, kissing him on the cheek. "Thanks for coming."

After the photo session, Megan said to her grandparents: "It's the interval so we're putting on some quiet music – the sort that you like."

"Does that mean we can eat now?" asked Joe.

"No, it doesn't!" said Anita, "Let's sit and listen to the music."

"There'll be nothing left after all these young vultures have finished," grumbled Joe.

"Don't be unkind, Joe. They're a nice crowd."

Joe sighed. Then suddenly the strains of Glenn Miller assailed their ears and they turned to each other: "Moonlight Serenade!" they cried.

"Do you remember how we used to dance to this at the Palace Ballroom, Joe?"

"How could I forget? You were a great dancing partner."

"Oh Joe," said Anita, with tears in her eyes.

"Shall we dance?"

Megan and her friends were clapping and whistling. Joe stopped, looking embarrassed.

"Oh, don't stop, Pop! You're still a great mover."

"Are you glad you came, Joe?" asked Anita.

"Yes I am," said Joe, holding her tighter." You know, you've hardly changed a bit since the first time I asked you to dance."

"Oh, go on with you," Anita giggled.

"I love you very much, old girl. Don't ever forget that."

"No, Joe, I won't. Now, let's have something to eat, I think you've earned it."

February 2007

Thursday

1

Friday

2

Saturday

3

Sunday

4

Monday

5

Tuesday

6
Accession Day
(Anniversary of Elizabeth II's accession in 1952)

Wednesday

7

Thursday

8

Friday

9

Saturday

10

Sunday

11

Monday

12

Tuesday

13

Wednesday

14
Valentine's Day

Thursday

15

Friday

16
Cheltenham Folk Festival begins

Saturday

17

Sunday

18
Chinese New Year (Year of the Pig)

Monday

19

Tuesday

20
Shrove Tuesday (Pancake Day)

Wednesday

21
Ash Wednesday (Lent begins)

Thursday

22

Friday 23	**Monday** 26
Saturday 24	**Tuesday** 27
Sunday 25	**Wednesday** 28

A Valentine

If I could paint a picture of
The love I feel for you,
I'd fill it with a blackbird's song,
A song so sweet and true.
I'd paint the magic of night skies
When bright stars wink and shine,
The wonder of a spider's web,
So strong and yet so fine;
The miracle of life itself,
The fragrance of a flower,
Sweet thoughts of you that fill my mind
With every passing hour.
And I would paint the pureness of
A tiny flake of snow.
A snowflake melts, but does my love?
Oh no, my darling, no.
My love for you is strong and true,
Believe me when I say,
I love you, and I always will,
For ever and a day.

Mrs Kay Spurr,
Kirkby Stephen, Cumbria

PIC: GLORIA H. CHOMICA/MASTERFILE

Above: Laurence and Evelyn on their wedding day in 1934
Left: Laurence in 1972
Centre: Doreen and her father in 1977

My Dad

My Dad, Laurence Staniforth, was born in Lincoln but regarded himself as a Yorkshireman, going to Goole Board School, then working as a miner in the South Yorkshire coalfields. These were hard times and Dad, especially protective towards his hard-done mother, left school at 13 in 1920.

Against the will of his hard-drinking, gambling father, and to the astonishment of the colliery official who wanted to train him as a deputy, Dad, newly converted to the Salvation Army, went to London in 1929 to train as an officer. At Sunderland, where he had his first appointment, he met my mother, Evelyn, who was about to begin her training. They married in 1934.

Although poorly educated, he was widely read. He used a natural talent for teaching young people, forming singing groups, writing dramas and raising money.

Before he was called up as a radar instructor, Dad had been an air raid warden, and after the war he became a Salvation Army supply preacher. I recall him rescuing and taking over from a badly heckled preacher at Speakers' Corner, Hyde Park.

After the war, just before the birth of my sister, Gwen, in 1946, Dad, without any technical training, borrowed library books and ordered materials.

Singlehanded, he broke through the kitchen into the washhouse to make a bathroom, and smashed through the yard concrete to lay piping for an indoor water supply with an immersion heater.

He taught me to draw, to row, to paint a door. I remember his flair for comedy and his singing of Trees; his devotion to my mother and his support for me and my sons right up to the eve of his death.

Doreen Simm, Sunderland

Meet my pet

Bobby, my Chihuahua, always listened for my neighbour to come out into her garden, as she used to cook him bacon rinds.

Dorothea M Abbott, Stratford-upon-Avon

Bobby, waiting for his favourite tit-bit!

Your February health

Keep warm and boost your circulation by staying as active as possible – a brisk walk, swinging your arms, is one of the best ways to stop blood flow getting sluggish (wrap up warm in lots of layers, especially if you have a circulation problem like Raynaud's disease). Give circulation an extra boost with the herb red vine leaf, shown to help strengthen blood vessels. Ask for it in your local health food store.

Healthy herbs
Harvesting your herbs

- It's important that herbs are picked at the correct time * Pick leaves while young and fresh – those produced after flowering are less desirable. Leaves from evergreens can be picked all year round.
- Harvest flowers as they appear, which may be anytime between spring and autumn depending on the plant. Choose those which haven't opened fully.
- Harvest seeds from late summer onwards and berries when they've ripened on the plant.
- Dig up roots as the leafy growth is just starting to die back.

Recipe of the week
Tangy Mushroom & Tomato Casserole

(Serves 4)

- 500 g (1 lb 2oz) blewit and horse mushrooms (Use closed cup mushrooms if exotic mushrooms aren't available)
- 2 red peppers, de-seeded and sliced
- 125 g (4½ oz) green beans, halved
- 6 shallots, halved
- 350 ml (12 fl oz) light vegetable stock
- 200 ml (7 fl oz) dry white wine
- 30 ml (2 tablespoons) tomato purée
- 3 cloves garlic, crushed
- 15 ml (1 tablespoon) fresh tarragon, torn
- Salt and pepper

1 Preheat oven to 190°C, 375°F, or Gas Mark 5.
2 Put all the vegetables in a large, deep ovenproof dish with lid.
3 Combine vegetable stock, white wine, tomato purée, garlic, tarragon, salt and pepper and pour over vegetables.
4 Cook in the oven for 20 minutes until vegetables are firm but cooked. Serve with cous cous.

RECIPE COURTESY THE VEGETARIAN SOCIETY

Top of the hit parade!

30 Jan 1959:
Elvis Presley
I Got Stung / One Night

30 Jan 1964:
Searchers
Needles & Pins

4 Feb 1965:
Righteous Brothers
You've Lost That Loving Feeling

Well I never...

The historical character who has been represented most often on screen is Napoleon Bonaparte – the role has been played in at least 194 films.

Top Tip

To loosen your cold hot water bottle stopper, run hot water over it and when the rubber softens it will be easier to undo.
J Oleskin, Apperly Bridge

Recipe of the week

Chocolate Orange Heart Cake

- 75 ml (3 fl oz) sunflower oil
- 75 ml (3 fl oz) orange flavoured yoghurt
- 3 tablespoons Seville orange marmalade
- 75 g (3 oz) Billington's Unrefined Muscovado sugar
- 2 eggs
- 110 g (4 oz) self-raising flour
- 1 tablespoon cocoa powder
- ½ teaspoon bicarbonate of soda

For the ganache
- 175 ml (6 fl oz) double cream
- 175 g (6 fl oz) plain chocolate
- Candied orange peel to decorate (optional)

1 Beat together the oil, yoghurt, marmalade, sugar and eggs in a large bowl. Sift together the dry ingredients and stir into the cake mixture.
2 Spoon into a greased lined 15cm heart shaped or round deep cake tin. Bake for 30-40 minutes at 170°C, 325°F, or Gas Mark 3, until a skewer comes out clean.
3 Cool in the tin for 10 minutes then turn out on to a wire rack to become cold.
4 Bring the cream to the boil in a pan. Add the chocolate and remove from the heat. Stir until smooth and cool for 5 minutes. Whisk the ganache until glossy and beginning to thicken.
5 Pour over the cake and spread with a palette knife over the sides. Leave to set but don't put the cake in the 'fridge or the ganache will become dull. Decorate with strips of candied orange peel.

RECIPE COURTESY BILLINGTON'S

Healthy herbs

Herbs and pets

How many of us have seen our dogs chewing grass when they're feeling unwell? Like many wild animals, they turn to plants when sickly. Although it's important that you only use small amounts and take really ill pets to the vet, if you follow the recommendations of herbal experts such as Jekka McVicar, there are homemade remedies such as this one for flea powder, that you can try yourself. Simply mix dried rosemary and wormwood with fennel seeds and rub them into your pet's coat.

Well I never…

Did you know that a 'fer de lance' is a large and venomous snake which comes from tropical South America?

Top Tip

When tightening and loosening screws always remember, 'Left is loose, Right is tight'.
Ethel Pickett, Tottenham

My Dad

In the 1950s my Dad, Les, was a signalman on Southern Railways. He used to cycle to and from his signal box – about six miles – in all weathers.

He would work long hours and arrive home after a night shift longing for his bed. My sister Lesley and I would jump into bed with him and pester him for the latest instalment of Harry Hedgehog, who lived next to his signal box and who would go up to the box for tea and biscuits (or so we thought!)

Later my younger sister,

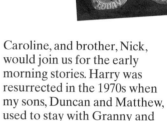

Above and right: Les enjoying his 80th birthday with his family

Caroline, and brother, Nick, would join us for the early morning stories. Harry was resurrected in the 1970s when my sons, Duncan and Matthew, used to stay with Granny and Granddad.

Every moment spent with our lovely Dad is so precious – all of us love him to bits!

Denise Graham, Alton, Hants

That special song

Even after nearly three years, the song Let It Be still brings tears to my eyes, and memories of sadness and love. As a teenager in the 1960s, The Beatles were my passion, and the love of my life was Paul McCartney. Life, of course, marched on, the children grew up and left home, leaving a void – to be filled by a puppy… Macs the Westie became a much adored and thoroughly spoiled member of the family – the cutest, funniest, most adorable dog there ever was. Life marched on for him, too, and eventually at the age of 16, we knew he'd had enough. A heartrending call was made to the local vet, who would come to our house at 4pm. I checked the clock for the hundredth time as Macs dozed on and off in his bed. But at 3pm, I bent down to stroke him and he looked at me with tired eyes as if to say, 'It's okay, I'm ready'. As I cradled him in my arms, the opening bars of Let It Be filled the air, and the tears flowed. I could never replace him, I am content to let it be.

Carol Gunstone, Bungay, Suffolk

Carol and Macs enjoying the beach

Macs the Westie

Healthy herbs

Discover more...

Called the 'Queen of Herbs' by Jamie Oliver, and a regular gold medal winner at The RHS Chelsea Royal Flower Show, Jekka McVicar knows everything there is to know about herbs. If these weekly ideas tempt you into discovering more, then buy her latest book, **New Book of Herbs**, which covers growing and using herbs in cooking, medicine and around the home – you'll soon be making up all your household cleaners, spicing up your cooking and enjoying a wonderfully scented garden.

Offer **Yours** readers can buy it for only £10.99 (RRP£12.99). To order please call the DK Bookshop on tel: 08700 707 717 quoting reference YY/NBH & ISBN 1405305797. Please allow up to 14 working days for delivery. Offer open to UK residents only, subject to availability. Offer ends February 28, 2007 and includes FREE P&P.

Top Tip

Keep a coin near your front door so you're not caught out when the charity collectors knock.

P Perry, Helston

Dear Diary

September 9, 1950

It was the first Holy Year since the end of the war, and my step-father had paid for me to go to Rome with a party of girls from my convent school. I was 16.

After lunch we were told to put on our school uniforms, as we were going to have a public audience with the Pope (Pius X). Although the temperature was in the high 80s we had to wear our full winter uniform – navy serge dresses with white collars and cuffs. Also lisle stockings, straw hats and white gloves.

We went to St Peter's Square, waiting outside we nearly got crushed to death. When we went inside, the air was foul because it was so hot and everybody was sweating.

At 6pm, the chandeliers were lit and showed up the gold ceiling. The effect was marvellous and amid 80,000 cheers, the Vatican guards in the picturesque red, gold and black uniforms advanced with the Pope in white, held up in a chair by four special guards with gold helmets...

Pat Clarke, Dartford, Kent

Nuns overseeing us on the beach in Italy, 1950, for a rare leisure period

---

Well I never...

Violins are made out of around 70 different parts, and are usually cut from wood that's aged for eight to ten years.

My Dad

My Dad was a dad in a million – always willing to lend a hand. He had lots of patience and was a very proud father on my wedding day.

Maureen Thayre, Kirriemuir, Angus

Maureen on her wedding day in February 1961 on the arm of her dad, William, with sisters Mary (in the middle) and Trudy on hand to deal with a blowaway veil

Recipe of the week

Pork Korma Chapatti
(Serves 2)
- 225 g (8 oz) lean pork fillet
- 15 ml (1 tablespoon) korma mild curry paste
- 15ml (1 tablespoon) crème fraîche
- 50 g (2 oz) baby spinach
- 30 ml (2 tablespoons) torn fresh coriander
- Chapattis
- Mango chutney

1 Cut the pork fillet into thin slices or strips, and dry fry in a hot non-stick wok for 5-6 minutes.
2 Add the korma mild curry paste and cook for 1-2 minutes. Add the crème fraîche, baby spinach and coriander leaves.
3 Pile into warmed chapattis, roll up and serve with a dollop of mango chutney

RECIPE COURTESY BRITISH MEAT

Meet my pet

A poem about Charlie, the African Grey parrot:

I'm searching for a tasty morsel,
Something like a nut.
There's heaps of toasted wheatflakes
And some plump sultanas, but
A crispy, roasted hazelnut
Is what I really crave.
If you could find one for me, mum,
I promise to behave.
Now, here's the deal, you help me
Then I'll go back to my cage.

I'm sure my eyesight's going,
Do you think it is my age?
Although I'm only 25
It could be I need glasses
To find nuts would be easy then,
I'd probably find masses.
But what's this under all these oats?
Look here, there's quite a stack,
And as I found them all myself,
I take my promise back!

Kay Spurr,
Kirkby
Stephen,
Cumbria

Charlie, the parrot – and he's peckish!

Recipe of the week

Luxury Bread and Butter Pudding

(Serves 4)

- 110 g (4 oz) slightly stale fruit loaf or brioche
- 50 g (2 oz) butter
- 4 tablespoons bitter orange or ginger marmalade
- 300 ml (½ pint) single cream
- 1 teaspoon vanilla extract
- 3 egg yolks
- 50 g (2 oz) Golden Caster sugar

1 Preheat the oven to 150°C, 300°F, or Gas Mark 2.
2 Slice the bread and spread first with the butter, then two tablespoons marmalade.
3 Slice diagonally in half and arrange in a buttered baking dish, spread side down.
4 Heat the cream to boiling point, then remove from the heat and stir in the vanilla extract.
5 Whisk the egg yolks with the sugar and pour on the cream, whisking all the time.
6 Strain over the bread and leave to soak for 2 hours.
7 Place the dish in a roasting tin and pour in enough hot water to come halfway up the sides of the dish.
8 Bake for 40-45 minutes until set. Remove from the oven and brush with the remaining marmalade.

RECIPE COURTESY BILLINGTON'S

Healthy herbs

Mint

Mint is one of our most popular herbs and is used in cooking, whether with new potatoes, as a salad garnish or in a glass of Pimm's and lemonade. Simple to grow, it should always be planted in a container because it can become invasive. There are many different varieties and their scents include spearmint, peppermint, applemint, pineapplemint and ginger mint. It grows best in moist soils and can be propagated by cuttings or division. Pick the fresh leaves and use immediately. Botanical name – *mentha*

■ **Tip:** When picking and drying the leaves, harvest just as flowering begins.

My Dad

There are so many things I remember about my much loved Dad, Frederick, including his love and support. However, there are two things that stand out in my memory in particular.

When there was an air raid over London in the night, he would come into my bedroom, wrap me in a blanket and take me down into the cellar. When the all-clear came, he would tuck me up tightly in bed and would plump up the pillow round my head, so I felt completely safe.

Also, the mingled smell of cigarettes and boot polish. He'd have a cigarette in his mouth and would polish his shoes, getting ready to take me, Mum and my brother for an evening out at the pictures. Sadly he is no longer with us but is still very much loved.

Barbara Boardman,
Weston-Super-Mare

Left: Barbara and her father by the air-raid shelter in 1940

Above: Barbara's late father, Fred, on his 90th birthday in 2004

Well I never...

'Children begin by loving their parents. After a while they judge them. Rarely, if ever, do they forgive them'.

Oscar Wilde

That special song

It all happened one day in 1948, the day I became engaged. Arriving at the jewellers, we chose a ring but it was too big, so left it there to be made into the right size.

We thought we'd while away the time at the nearby cinema, The Forum in Bath (now long gone as a cinema).

We arrived just in time for the matinee, as the house lights were still up. Ravel's Bolero was playing, but we thought it a bit strange that when the record finished, it started again. Obviously there was a bit of a problem in the projection room because we heard it four times!

Eventually it was sorted out because the lights dimmed, we watched the film and then rushed back to the jewellers. The ring? A perfect fit!

And now, 58 years on, when we hear Bolero we think of the significance that the tune has had on our marriage.

Nancy Hillyer, Trowbridge, Wilts

Top of the hit parade!

23 Feb 1961:
Petula Clark
Sailor

22 Feb 1962:
Elvis Presley
Can't Help Falling In Love /
Rock-A-Hula Baby

23 Feb 1974:
Suzi Quatro
Devil Gate Drive

Places to visit

On location at Burghley House

Modern sculpture, medieval splendour

Along with the nearby picturesque town of Stamford, Burghley House is a popular destination for TV and film crews. Both the town and the great house are built in a distinctive stone from a local quarry in Northamptonshire.

The park at Burghley House housed more than 30 trailers and 300 crew when The Da Vinci Code was shot there. The house represented Castile Gandolfo and the grounds were used to shoot additional scenes set in the French countryside.

Other films featuring Burghley include Pride and Prejudice (in which it portrays Rosings, home of Lady Catherine de Bourgh, played by Dame Judi Dench) and The Golden Bowl, starring Nick Nolte and Uma Thurman.

One of the grandest houses dating from the Elizabethan era, it was built for the Queen's Lord High Treasurer, William Cecil, who was also responsible for much of the design. However, his duties at court meant he was unable to live in the house on a permanent basis. Today, Burghley remains a family home, lived in by Lady Victoria Leatham, a descendant of the first Lord Burghley.

Over the centuries, the house has seen many changes. In the seventeenth century, the open loggias around the ground floor were enclosed and two centuries later a two-storey corridor was constructed around the inner courtyard to provide space for modern innovations such as bathrooms. The grounds, which are home to a herd of fallow deer, were landscaped by 'Capability' Brown who supervised the demolition of the house's northwest wing to give a better view of the parkland.

Although the house does not open before April, the Sculpture Garden is open all year. Covering 15 acres, the garden features fascinating contemporary sculptures in a natural setting.

■ *For further information, phone 01780 752451 or visit website www.burghley.co.uk*

Remember when...
Carrying a torch

Vera Hilton of Selby, Yorkshire, loved life as an usherette

Much to my mother's annoyance – she wanted me to do office work – when I was 15, back in the 1930s, I answered an advert to be an usherette in a small cinema called the Clapham Pavilion. I became one of the girls with a large torch who showed people to their seats. In the intervals, with heavy trays strung around our necks, we called out: 'Teas, chocolates, cigarettes'.

I was very happy in my work and after a while I was promoted to the cash desk and sat in a little box selling tickets. I loved meeting lots of different people; making cups of tea for elderly customers in the afternoons and keeping the children in order on Saturdays. The children were full of fun and laughter and no cheek – they behaved when I spoke to them.

Our hours were from 1.30pm to 9pm so it would often be dark when I walked home alone, about half an hour's walk, but there was no fear and no vandals in those days.

Vera (second from left) in 1933 on the roof of the cinema

We worked on Sundays but had one day off a week. When I became a cashier I received 15s a week and was able to open my own post office account in which I saved one shilling a week. Sometimes I'd get a tip for making a cup of tea or people would say, 'Keep the change', and I was over the moon.

When I married and left work, I missed it all – office work was not for me!

It was...
the night of the duck

Alex Barzdo rescued a poor little quacker one stormy night – and rather wished he hadn't

To get to our little bungalow cottage at Detling, in Kent, it was necessary to pass between the village school and a neighbour's house. This night had been very stormy and, as we came home late, very tired and rather wet, we were all keen to get into the dry, have a cup of tea and flop into a warm bed. There were no streetlights on in the village after ten o'clock, so we used torches to find our way up the dark pathway to our garden gate.

However there was something else there in the dark, also feeling rather the worse for wear in the terrible weather. As we passed by our neighbour's car, we heard a faint but distressed little quacking.

I bent down and flashed the torch under the car and saw a small duck. As I peered beneath the wheel arch, it blinked a little in the sudden light of the torch, which I'd put down beside me.

A young mallard, having lost his way, was sheltering from the storm under my neighbour's car. We felt so sorry for it that we decided to take it in for the night, out of the blasts of the icy rain wreaking havoc on the Kentish landscape.

On my hands and knees on the gravel path, I reached under the car and surprisingly the duck put up no fuss as I tucked it up in a car blanket. Then we had to think how to accommodate Wellington (named by my daughter) in our small cottage.

While we got ready for bed, I found a couple of old towels and laid them in a spare washing-up bowl in a corner of the hall. Wellington seemed quite comfy there, evidently pleased to be out of the howling winds, and settled to a bit of preening, with satisfied mallard-type noises.

After the bedtime wash-teeth-and-toilet routine, I decided it would be fairest for all of us (including Wellington) to be shut in his towel 'nest', in the bathroom.

It was then I had a brainwave.

A brainwave when you're tired is not always the smartest thing, but it did seem a good idea at the time. It was... for the duck. I half-filled the bath with water for our visitor to enjoy before we awoke.

We all slept soundly – until about 6am. What a racket – I never knew that ducks could make such a din! Probably enjoying the echo in the bathroom, as I suppose we do when we sing in the bath.

When we went in to see our feathered friend, he was having a whale of a time diving into the bathwater time and again. Accompanied by very loud quacking, he was drenching every area of his new home with vigorous splashing from half-extended wings. Absolutely everything in the room was soaking! Everything! Walls and cupboards were running with water, towels and rugs were sodden, the low ceiling was dripping. It was going to take weeks to dry this lot. There was nothing for it – Wellington had to get the boot!

I scrambled about and found an old box and stuffed an old dustsheet into the bottom. Then we rounded up Wellington who was sitting preening in his bedtime nest and bundled him unceremoniously, and with some name-calling, into his 'removal box'.

The rugs, towels and flannels went into the washer and, while my daughter and I carried Wellington to the car, my wife started on the mopping up operation.

So that's why, at 6.30 on a Sunday morning, a disgruntled and bleary-eyed parent and child were to be seen in Mote Park in Maidstone, releasing a duck from a cardboard box on the bank of the lake. And that's why in future, I'll always duck out of putting a mallard in my bath.

PIC: MASTERFILE

Thursday

1
St. David's Day

Friday

2
29th European Indoor Athletics Championships begins (National Indoor Arena)

Saturday

3

Sunday

4

Monday

5

Tuesday

6

Wednesday

7

Thursday

8
Crufts begins (National Exhibition Centre)

Friday

9

Saturday

10

Sunday

11
Opening ceremony ICC Cricket World Cup

Monday

12
Commonwealth Day

Tuesday

13

Wednesday

14
National No Smoking Day

Thursday

15

Friday

16

Saturday

17
St. Patrick's Day (Bank Holiday in N Ireland)

Sunday

18
Mothering Sunday

Monday

19

Tuesday

20

Wednesday

21

Thursday

22

Friday	Wednesday
23	28
Saturday	Thursday
24	29
Sunday	Friday
25 British Summer Time (BST) begins, Clocks go forward	30
Monday	Saturday
26	31
Tuesday	
27	

Snowdrops

Through frozen mounds of deep brown earth,
Between damp fallen leaves,
A mass of emerald shoots creep up
As silently as thieves.

And every day they thrive and reach
Towards the beckoning sun,
Awakened from their wintry sleep,
To see if spring's begun.

From slender stems white buds burst forth
And soon begin to swell.
Then petals spread their wings to form
The snowdrop's drooping bell.

They signal with their nodding heads
That winter's on the wane,
And warmer days are on their way
To cheer the earth again.

Jean Penn, Gosport, Hants

PIC: FRANK KRAHMER/MASTERFILE

Your March health

Don't ignore your feet just because they're crammed into shoes all the time at the moment. A few times a week, half fill a large bucket or basin with hot water and add several tablespoons of salt, stirring until it's dissolved. Then soak your feet for about 15 minutes. This helps keep the skin on your feet soft and tackles any infections around your nails.

Top of the hit parade!

2 Mar 1961:
Everly Brothers
Walk Right Back

27 Feb 1964:
Cilla Black
Anyone Who Had A Heart

2 Mar 1967:
Engelbert Humperdink
Release Me

Top Tip

A potato peeler used on a bar of cold cooking chocolate is ideal for making curls and twirls to decorate cakes.

Poppy 'boxing' clever!

Meet my pet

This is our dear cat Poppy, who was found in a cardboard box in 1990, and who came to us at nine weeks old. Just a little kitten, suffering from cat flu who was rescued by Cats Protection.

Poppy is very affectionate and great company, with a loud purr – she's also very demanding!

Her only claim to fame is her name, as our daughter couldn't make up her mind: Poppy, Henrietta, Thomasina, Clabose McCavity.

Priscilla Ann Hooker, Ilkeston

My Dad

My Dad was a typical working man who was exempt from becoming a soldier in the Second World War because he worked in a foundry making war weapons. As a child, I was only aware that he was either always at work or in bed.

When that terrible period finished (and by then I had two brothers) he took us out on day trips every weekend, despite never having a car. As long as there was a pub, he could pop into for a few pints while we sat outside with lemonade and crisps, our outings were made!

His humour was very dry and I remember him saying about a new boyfriend, 'I'm not worried about who you sleep with, just who you stay awake with!'

Unfortunately, he died at the early age of 55, worn out, I think, from his very hard job, but my brothers and sisters and I have lovely memories and photographs.

Audrey Gibbons, Birmingham

Audrey's Dad, Fred Newman

Healthy herbs

Rosemary

A mediterranean herb, rosemary has a spicy, resinous fragrance and is popular as a flavouring for meats and dressings – and may be used when garnishing a roast. It has lovely aromatic leaves and powder-blue flowers in early summer and thrives in a well-drained, sunny location. You can take cuttings or grow it from seed. Use fresh leaves as they're required. Botanical name – *Rosmarinus officinalis*.

■ **Tip:** If the plant outgrows its space, cut it back after flowering.

Well I never…

The largest cinema organ in the world was the Wurlitzer installed at Radio City Music Hall, New York, in 1932. Still in use, it has 58 ranks of pipes.

Recipe of the week

Beef and Sweet Pepper Quesadillas

(Serves 4)

■ 30 ml (2 tablespoons) oil
■ 2 cloves garlic, peeled and finely chopped
■ 2 spring onions, finely chopped
■ 1 red pepper, deseeded and finely chopped
■ 1 yellow pepper, deseeded and finely chopped
■ 375 g (13 oz) beef mince
■ 100 g (4 oz) chorizo sausage, roughly cubed
■ Large pinch chilli flakes
■ Salt and freshly milled black pepper
■ 30-45 ml (2-3 tablespoons) freshly chopped coriander or flat leaf parsley
■ 1 x 326 g pack flour tortillas
■ 60 ml (4 tablespoons) tomato chutney
■ 1 x 150 g tub or bag buffalo mozzarella cheese, roughly torn

1 Heat half the oil in a large shallow, non-stick frying pan and cook the garlic, onions and peppers for 1-2 minutes.
2 Add the mince and chorizo and cook for 5-10 minutes until brown. Stir in the chilli flakes and season. Add the coriander or parsley and cool slightly.
3 Place 4 tortillas on a chopping board and spread evenly with the chutney, beef and cheese. Top each with another tortilla, press down and set aside.
4 Heat the remaining oil in a clean, non-stick frying pan on a moderate heat and fry the tortillas, one at a time for 2-3 minutes. Invert onto a plate, then slide back into the pan and cook for a further 2-3 minutes until the cheese melts.
5 Repeat with the remaining tortillas, adding extra oil to the pan if required.
6 Slice into quarters and serve immediately.

RECIPE COURTESY OF QUALITY STANDARD BEEF

Well I never…

It was once law to say 'God bless you' to someone who sneezed.

Recipe of the week

No Bake Chocolate Cake

(Serves 6-8)

- 200 g (7 oz) milk chocolate, broken into pieces
- 100 g (approx 3 1/2 oz) plain chocolate (at least 60% cocoa solids), broken into pieces
- 110 g (4 oz) unsalted butter
- 50 g (2 oz) unrefined dark muscovado sugar
- 110 g (4 oz) shortbread biscuits, broken into small pieces
- 110 g (4 oz) glacé cherries, halved
- 75 g (3 oz) whole roasted hazelnuts
- 75 g (3 oz) pecan nuts, roughly chopped
- 1 small packet white Maltesers, crushed roughly
- Chocolate mini eggs to decorate (optional)

1 Melt the chocolate, butter and sugar in a bowl over a pan of simmering (not boiling) water or in a microwave oven.
2 Leave to cool but not starting to set. Stir in the rest of the ingredients.
3 Turn into an 18 cm round cake tin lined with non-stick baking paper, pressing down gently. Decorate with chocolate mini eggs if using. Leave to set at room temperature until firm.
4 Remove the cake from the tin and peel away the lining paper. Cut into thin slices to serve.

RECIPE COURTESY BILLINGTON'S

Healthy herbs

Sage

Great as groundcover because it is colourful and tends to sprawl, sage is a woody, hardy perennial. Pick the leaves as required and use when stuffing poultry, rabbit and pork. Although the plants can be cut back during the spring as buds break from the base, they're best renewed every three years – you can do this by sowing seed or taking cuttings. Botanical name – *Salvia officinalis*
■**Tip:** Choose the variety 'Tricolor' because it has striking green, cream and purple leaves.

Top Tip

Put a drop of room freshener in your humidifier to freshen up your room.

Top of the hit parade!

Left: Joyce's dad, Jim, in uniform in 1949
Above: Jim's motorbike and sidecar

My Dad

My Dad Jim was in the Metropolitan Police for 31 years. We were living in Richmond, Surrey at the time. When I was 10, he was knocked off his cycle and broke his leg. The surgeon said to him, 'You should never have been in this job, should you?'

My Dad knew what he meant as he had broken the other leg and had shrapnel in it from the First World War. My Dad had never told the police authority, and they'd never picked it up at his medical.

I was 12 when he retired and he stayed on as a civilian and went out daily to clean the police telephone boxes (the Tardis) on his motor cycle and sidecar. After a while Dad bought a little Morris 8 – we were the first in the street to have a car and he kept it in the front garden.

Joyce Gale, Bristol

That special song

In September 1935 I was one of three bridesmaids at my sister's wedding. We wore pale blue silk dresses, large picture hats, and carried lovely bouquets of pink carnations.

My boyfriend, Arthur, had a lovely tenor voice, and used to sing in an amateur operatic society – Gilbert and Sullivan mostly. But on my sister's wedding day, he sang Softly Awakes My Heart from Samson and Delilah, and You Are My Heart's Desire as sung by Richard Tauber.

Arthur looked at me most of the time he was singing; I was 19 and he was 24. Although I am almost 90 now and Arthur died in 1982, I still think about that magical day in 1935. We married the following year, in December 1936.

Millicent Shovelton, Ferndown, Dorset

Left: Millicent in 1933

Left: Kelpie and her puppies having a tug of war
Below: Kelpie sitting to attention

Dear Diary

Mothering Sunday weekend, 2004

Beryl with daughter Janet and son Jeff

I'll never forget that weekend, as I was recovering from a knee replacement in a Belgium Hospital. I'd had the operation the Wednesday before and was feeling very sorry for myself and far from home with no visitors, having had a painful morning.

Later, a man popped his head round the door and I was struck as to how much he looked like my son, Jeff. A lady followed him and, lo and behold, it was my son and daughter – with a huge bunch of flowers!

Everyone had been sworn to secrecy, even my youngest grandson, then aged seven. They stayed overnight and came to see me again on Mothering Sunday. It gave me the lift I needed and I am sure, helped my speedy recovery.

Beryl M Kelsey, Upminster

Top Tip

A large empty coffee jar will hold a packet of wire wool pads and stop them drying out.

J Batchelor

Meet my pet

We have a Jack Russell called Kelpie who came from a rescue centre. Our local vet checked her over, who said she had no fleas and was not pregnant – so far, so good!

She went into kennels some weeks later when we went on holiday, so we were keen to see her on our return. I was so surprised when my husband returned without Kelpie and said, 'You're a granny to two pups!'

We brought them home and Kelpie was a great mother; she carried them about in her mouth. The pups were hard work but lots of fun and we managed to find homes for them. Kelpie was spayed to make sure there were no more surprises!

She has been a great friend to us both and loves playing football in the garden.

Maylyn Hanley, Carrickfergus, Co Antrim

Well I never…

'Money frees you from doing things you dislike. Since I dislike doing nearly everything, money is handy.'

Groucho Marx (1890 – 1977)

Healthy herbs

Summer savory

Not commonly grown by gardeners, summer savory is a tender annual with white or lavender flowers. Its spicy leaves are popular as a condiment with meat and vegetables. Pick the young leaves and use fresh or hang in an airy, shaded place until crisp and dry. The leaves are antibacterial, antifungal and antiseptic. Sow seed in pots on a windowsill during spring and plant out at the end of May.
Botanical name – *Satureja hortensis*
■**Tip:** Add it to bean dishes and it

Top of the hit parade!

12 Mar 1954:
Stargazers
I See The Moon

16 Mar 1956:
Dream Weavers
It's Almost Tomorrow

14 Mar 1963:
Cliff Richard
Summer Holiday

My Dad

For many years, my father, Percy's, hobby was roses. Our front garden always looked very attractive in the summer with various colour blooms and the large back garden was full of rose bushes.

In those days, I knew the name of each rose but I didn't know the names of other flowers and had to ask people what they were.

My father died in 1970; sadly the current trend is to concrete over front gardens for car parking – more practical but not so colourful!

Marie Le Lacheur, Aldershot, Hants

Percy Le Lacheur tending his roses, around 1950

Recipe of the week

Spicy Lamb Naan with Cucumber and Lime Dollop

(Serves 2)
- 225 g (8oz) lean lamb leg steaks
- 5 ml (1 teaspoon) ground cumin
- 5 ml (1 teaspoon) ground coriander
- 5 ml (1 teaspoon) olive oil
- 1 red onion, thinly sliced
- 2 cloves garlic, crushed
- 5 cherry tomatoes, halved

For the Cucumber and Lime Dollop
- 30ml (2tbsp) crème fraîche
- ¼ cucumber
- Juice and rind from ½ lime
- Naan bread

1 Take the lamb and cut into thin strips. Sprinkle with the ground coriander and ground cumin

2 Heat the olive oil in a griddle or frying pan and add the red onion and garlic. Cook for 1-2 minutes and then add the lamb strips. Cook for 3-4 minutes.

3 Add the cherry tomatoes, and cook for 1-2 minutes until just softened.

4 Meanwhile make the Cucumber and Lime Dollop. Mix together the crème fraîche with the chopped cucumber and lime rind and juice.

5 Heat the naan bread in the oven for 2-3 minutes until warmed through and soft. Spoon the lamb mix into the centre of the naan bread, add a spoonful of cucumber and lime dollop and carefully fold in the edges.

RECIPE COURTESY BRITISH MEAT

Recipe of the week

Hot Cross Buns

(Makes 12)

- 450 g (1 lb) strong white flour
- 1 teaspoon salt
- 1 teaspoon dried cinnamon
- 1 teaspoon mixed spice
- 50 g (2 oz) butter
- 2 teaspoons powdered/easy blend dried yeast
- 85 g (approx 3 oz) mixed dried fruit or raisins or sultanas
- Zest from one lemon (or orange if preferred)
- 25 g (1 oz) Fruisana Fruit Sugar
- 8 fl oz milk
- 1 egg

Crosses:
- 4 tablespoons flour
- 4 tablespoons water

Glaze:
- 2 tablespoons Fruisana Fruit Sugar
- 4 tablespoons milk

1 Sift the flour, salt and spices into a large bowl. Rub in the butter. Stir in dried fruit, yeast, lemon zest and Fruisana.
2 Warm the milk in a saucepan and whisk in the egg. Mix well with the flour mixture and bring together into a ball.
3 Flour a flat surface and knead the dough for 10 minutes. Divide into 12 balls.
4 Place balls on a baking tray, cover and leave to rise in a warm place for 1 - 2 hours until they double in size.

Crosses:
1 Mix the flour with enough of the water to make a thick batter – use a piping bag or carefully drizzle across each bun.
2 Bake for 20-30 minutes at 190 C, 375 F, Gas Mark 5.

Glaze:
Heat the milk and Fruisana until dissolved. Brush each bun two or three times while they cool on a wire rack.

RECIPE COURTESY FRUISANA

Healthy herbs

Borage

Borage has been used for centuries – Celtic warriors even painted themselves with it, believing it brought courage – and it still has its uses. Its flowers and leaves taste rather like cucumber so are worth adding to salads – the flowers are extremely pretty and will become a talking point when entertaining. Botanical name – *Borago officinalis*

- **Tip:** Add a few leaves to your meals if you're feeling low, because it should lift your spirits

My Dad

The memory I hold most dear of my Dad was of him holding his silver cup with the inscription on the base stand which said:

To Oliver Cook
In recognition of 50 years
uninterrupted
Service to the Brass Band
Movement

He was a cornet player and a coal miner and was in Bolsover Colliery Silver Prize Band and in his later years, Eckington Miners' Welfare Band. He wrote music and taught many young musicians who were in junior bands.

When I was a little girl I remember loving Sunday mornings when the house would

Oliver Cook, (2nd from right) with other band members at a concert in Skegness in the late 1940s

resound with the men practising the quartets in our front room. He was in his eighties when he retired from his music.

I heard a lovely piece of music once and told him it was Solveig's Song from the Peer Gynt Suite. He liked it so much he used to play it for his cornet solo each time they held a concert.

He was known as a very melodious player and said that the secret was to rinse a pint

of milk several times through his cornet, then rinse with cold water, which would give it the lovely tone.

When he was 11 years old, he won the Open Championship of Great Britain for the best solo cornet player in his age group in the slow melody section.

A lovely, quiet, gentle man and a wonderful musician – my Dad, Oliver Cook.

Eileen Newman,
Bolsover, Derbys

That special song

My husband and I have a special song – Kitty Kallen singing Little Things Mean A Lot. In 1956 and 1957, her record was played regularly on the radio, so it soon became 'our' song.

We courted for many years, Derek and I, during which time he served in Japan doing his National Service, and we were apart for more than a year.

We married in 1958 and now three children and eight grandchildren later, we are still happily married.

Marion Mottram, Rochdale

Left: Marion and Derek on their wedding day in 1958
Right: Marion and Derek today – mind that seagull, Derek!

Well I never…

Elvis Presley once worked at a trucking company that was owned by Frank Sinatra.

Top of the hit parade!

20 Mar 1959:
The Platters
Smoke Gets In Your Eyes

23 Mar 1961:
Elvis Presley
Wooden Heart

22 Mar 1962:
Shadows
Wonderful Land

My Dad

My Dad, Sidney, was a man of few words; he read widely and could always answer the umpteen questions I asked him. He had been all round the world in the Merchant Navy and during the First World War had been stationed at Cork, St Kilda and Stornoway in the Outer Hebrides, where he met my mother.

After the war, he and a naval colleague set up a radio shop in Birmingham, one of only two there at the time. It was the early days of wireless and once when Dad had brought home a radio, our elderly neighbours were invited in to listen to it. The old man was so astonished, he dropped down on all fours and crawled round the room looking under the furniture for the source of the voice!

A very caring Dad, he once took the last bus into Birmingham to meet me off the midnight train from London and walk with me the four miles back home – and I took it all for granted.

Dorothea Abbott, Stratford-Upon-Avon

Dorothea enjoying a donkey ride with her dad, Sidney

Top Tip

Any junk mail you receive with nothing printed on the back can be cut into strips and used as notepads and shopping lists.

K Rawthson, Penrith

Well I never...

Give a man a fish and he eats for a day. Teach him how to fish and you get rid of him all weekend.

Zenna Schaffer

Meet my pet

Meet Tammy, my West Highland White Terrier, who was two years old last February. She played with my slippers as a puppy, and used to sleep in one! She is strong willed, with a mind of her own but is terrific entertainment!

Marilyn Dunn, Eastbourne

Would you play with me please?

Healthy herbs

Chervil

Similar in appearance to parsley, but paler green in colour, chervil is a pretty annual with lacy leaves and flat heads of delicate white flowers. A hardy annual, it can be sown outside during early spring. Use the young leaves as you would parsley – as a garnish and in soups, sauces and all kinds of egg dishes, or cut and dry them. Botanical name – *Anthriscus cerefolium*

■ **Tip:** Sow chervil late in the year and it can be used instead of parsley during winter.

Top of the hit parade!

Recipe of the week

Lamb with Mint, Rosemary and Lime, with Dill and Lime Potatoes

(Serves 4-6)

Time to cook: Marinating time 4-5 hours + 30-40 minutes
Cooking temperature: Barbecue or gas mark 6, 200°C 400°F

- 1kg (2.5lb) lean leg of lamb fillet end (chunky top end of leg) boneless, strings removed and flattened out
- 15 ml (1 tablespoon) olive oil
- 3 cloves garlic, crushed
- 15 ml (1 tablespoon) fresh rosemary, chopped
- 1 tablespoon fresh mint, chopped
- Juice and rind of 1 lime
- 150 ml (¼ pint) white wine

For the Lime and Dill Potatoes

- 900g (2lb) new potatoes
- 30ml (2tablespoons) mayonnaise
- 30ml (2tablespoons) dill (if you can't get dill use basil)
- Juice of ½ lime
- ¼ cucumber, sliced

1 Take the leg fillet end, and cut it so that the meat can be flattered out (the lamb joint will be about 2-3 inches (5-8 cm) thick)
2 In a large dish place the olive oil, crushed garlic, rosemary, mint, lime rind and juice and the white wine. Mix together and add the flattered lamb, cover and leave to marinate in the refrigerator for 4-5 hours.
3 Drain and cook on a preheated barbecue (with lid) for 30-40 minutes so that the outside is golden and meat still pink inside, or alternatively cook in the oven directly on the cooking shelf with a drip tray below for about 30-40 minutes.

Lime & Dill Potatoes:

4 Boil new potatoes until tender, drain and cool, add the mayonnaise, lime juice, fresh dill and cucumber, sliced.
5 Serve lamb cut into thick chunks with potatoes, steamed green beans and a tomato balsamic salad.

RECIPE COURTESY BRITISH MEAT

Places to visit

On location at Pollok House

Glasgow's Georgian glory

Pollok House, claimed to be the Scottish country house at its best, appeared in the TV series Murder Rooms, starring Ian Richardson and Charles Dance, and was the location for the film Unleashed, starring Morgan Freeman and Bob Hoskins.

Situated at the heart of a thousand acre estate, the house is still within the Glasgow city boundaries and with its woodlands, rolling fields and golf courses provides a green lung for the townspeople. The courses date from the 1890s when the then owner, Sir John Stirling Maxwell, sought to preserve the open space from an encroaching city. The park is home to one of the best known herds of Highland cattle in Scotland,

known as the Pollok Fold.

A classic Georgian building, Pollok House was adapted and expanded sympathetically into a large Edwardian house with all the modern conveniences and luxuries. The best of the Georgian period is the exuberant plasterwork in the main rooms and the best of the later additions is the enormous suite of 42 rooms built to accommodate the army of servants needed to operate the house in its heyday. At weekends, the house is brought to life as 'servants' and 'family members' go about their business in period costume.

Art lovers will not want to miss a visit to the Stirling Maxwell Collection, featuring some of the best examples of Spanish paintings in Britain. It includes El Greco's The Lady in a Fur Wrap, the most famous work on display in the house.

It was at Pollok House in 1931 that Sir John and his friends decided to start a National Trust to preserve and care for Scotland's heritage in all its forms and the house is now managed by the National Trust for Scotland.

■ *For further information, phone 0141 616 6410 or visit the website nts.org.uk*

Remember when...
Getting over it

Valerie Burton of Oxford enjoyed convalescence

After being in hospital with rheumatic fever, I was admitted to Marlborough Children's Convalescent Home in Wiltshire. This had been the workhouse and was on the outskirts of the town. The wards were long, old-fashioned rooms with 12 beds, six on each side. Because my bed was on the left hand side, my doctor was a lovely man called Dr Dick, the right hand side had the less jovial Dr Balman.

I was at the far end next to the TV which, joy of joys, had ITV. At home we only had BBC, so I was able to see Bonanza, Bootsie and Snudge and early episodes of Coronation Street. The nurses lent us their record player and records so we

could listen to the latest pop music. I remember trying to keep awake on Sunday nights to listen to the hit parade on Radio Luxembourg on a radio that was muffled under someone's bedclothes.

I was a bed-rest patient for two weeks during which time I had physiotherapy to build up my muscles. Then I was able to sit on a chair for one hour a day for a week which was gradually extended until I was up for eight hours a day. When you reached five hours up per day, you were allowed to go to school in one of the two classrooms (one for primary and one for secondary school). Also, when you were up for five hours, you could have

Valerie was one happy patient

your meals in the canteen. I really enjoyed my stay, and grew up both mentally and physically. When my husband and I returned recently we found the site had been turned into luxury flats for the elderly. Talking to the caretaker, we learned of other ex-patients who had returned and also remembered their days there as happy ones.

The Fun Film Quiz

**Test your knowledge with these tricky teasers
– if you get stuck, the answers are at the bottom of the page.**

1 What film is the last musical to win the Oscar® for Best Picture?
a) Camelot
b) My Fair Lady
c) Oliver!
d) The Sound of Music

2 George Lazenby was Bond in which film
a) Thunderball
b) Living Daylights
c) Goldeneye
d) On Her Majesty's Secret Service

3 What was Marilyn Monroe's real name?
a) Jean Mary
b) Mary Jean
c) Norma Jean
d) Mary Norma

4 Which actress has been nominated for the most Oscars®?
a) Meryl Streep
b) Katharine Hepburn
c) Bette Davis
d) Ingrid Bergman

5 Which of Alfred Hitchcock's early works is credited as Britain's first full-length talkie?
a) Vertigo
b) The Lady Vanishes
c) The 39 Steps
d) Blackmail

6 Richard Attenborough plays the leader of a teen gang in Brighton Rock (1947). What is his character called?
a) Pinkie Brown
b) Georgie Brown
c) Slasher Brown
d) Gordon Brown

7 The 2004 remake of The Ladykillers featured Tom Hanks, but who took the lead role in the original 1955 Ealing comedy?
a) Cecil Parker
b) Herbert Lom
c) Alec Guinness
d) Peter Sellers

Richard Attenborough played a fresh-faced teen gangster

8 What is the title of the 1969 musical romp that featured the singing talents of Lee Marvin and Clint Eastwood?
a) Cat Ballou
b) Coogan's Bluff
c) Donovan's Reef
d) Paint Your Wagon

9 Which young actress played Spencer Tracy's daughter in Father of The Bride?
a) Audrey Hepburn
b) Elizabeth Taylor
c) Grace Kelly
d) Judy Garland

10 Who is Cary Grant's character in The Bishop's Wife?
a) The Bishop
b) A Parishioner
c) An Angel
d) A Priest

A winning smile
by Jean Pressling

Tom's addiction to entering competitions is getting on Gladys's nerves…

Gladys rolled out the pastry and was transferring it to her pie dish when she heard Tom's key in the lock. "Is that you, Tom?" she called.

"No, it's Hugh Grant," came the reply.

"Good," she said, ignoring his sarcasm, "You can come and open this tin of meat for me."

Tom walked over to the dresser where the tin-opener was kept. "Where is it then?"

"It's there – that tin with no label on it."

"You can't put that in a pie," declared Tom, "It's dog food."

Gladys was horrified. "Dog food," she shrieked. "Since when have we bought dog food? We've never had a dog."

"I bought it," admitted Tom. "There was a competition on the label. First prize was a television set."

"You and your ruddy competitions!" Gladys exploded. "I'm sick to death of having to guess what's inside the tins in my larder because you've removed the labels. You promised me you'd mark the tins after I nearly served up rice pudding on toast instead of baked beans."

"I did mark them, love," Tom protested, pushing the tin under her nose, "Look, SB for Sunny Boy."

"I thought that meant stewed beef," Gladys retorted. "That does it! You can go straight down to Mr Patel's and buy a tin of stewed beef and from now on you can confine your competition entries to those in magazines."

Over the next few days Gladys felt quite sorry for Tom when she saw him moping about the house with nothing to do. He hated gardening and he was hopeless at DIY, which was why he'd taken up competitions after retiring. He had spent hours hunched over his entry forms, trying to think up pithy slogans for everything from marmalade to soap powder.

But she was determined not to weaken. Not only was she sick of trying to guess the contents of unlabelled tins, she was also tired of having his competition paraphernalia spread over the dining table.

About a week later, it was Tom's turn to make the morning tea. Gladys heard him pottering about in the kitchen, then the sound of the postman delivering the mail. "More bills, I suppose," she muttered to herself.

"Gladys, I've done it! I've done it!" yelled Tom. Gladys shot out of bed and rushed downstairs to see what it was

that Tom had done. He was standing in the hall holding an envelope in his hand. It was typewritten and bore a well-known company logo.

"This is it, Glad," he smiled, "my first big win."

"What have you won, love?" Gladys gazed at her husband with new respect.

With trembling fingers he opened the envelope and read out: "Dear Mr Winslow, congratulations! We are delighted to inform you that you have won second prize in the Sunny Boy dog food competition. Your prize, a year's supply of Sunny Boy, will be delivered soon."

Gladys sat on the stairs and laughed until her sides ached. Tom couldn't see the funny side of it, though. He pushed past her and went upstairs to the bathroom. When he came down again he was dressed in his outdoor clothes.

"Where do you think you're going?" Gladys asked.

"Out!" snapped Tom.

"But you haven't had any breakfast."

"Don't want any," came the surly reply. The front door slammed shut.

Gladys finished her coffee and looked at her watch. Tom had been gone more than three hours and she was getting worried. Perhaps, she shouldn't have laughed so heartily.

> ## "I'm sick to death of having to guess what's inside the tins in my larder"

Supposing he'd had an accident…

The door bell rang and she rushed to open it. A sheepish looking Tom stood there: "Sorry, love; I forgot my key."

"Thank goodness you're all right. I was going frantic…" Her voice trailed off. "What on earth is that?" she stammered, staring at a scruffy lump of brown fur which seemed to be attached to Tom's hand.

"It's a dog."

"I can see it's a dog, but whose is it?"

"It's ours."

"Oh, no, Tom – please – you know I don't like dogs."

"Too bad," Tom said firmly, "He needs a home and we need a dog to eat up all that Sunny Boy. By the way, that's what I've called him – Sunny."

"But where did you find him?"

"At The Wanderers Pet Sanctuary; they found him living in an abandoned car. He was starving, poor thing. I don't think he'll laugh at the prize I won."

"Well, he'll be your responsibility," Gladys insisted, "I don't want anything to do with him – filthy looking creature."

Within weeks Sunny was part of the family. Tom spent hours grooming him and Gladys was forced to admit he was quite a handsome animal with his glossy chestnut coat and huge brown eyes. Tom was looking better, too; slimmer and more relaxed. Man and dog were inseparable; they walked for miles,

happy in each other's company.

"He might just as well be back at work for all I see of him these days," Gladys grumbled as she unpacked her shopping. She was putting a packet of cornflakes in the cupboard when the word 'competition' caught her eye…

When Tom and Sunny returned home, Gladys was busy with pen, notebook and dictionary. "Hello, love; I'm glad you're back. How would you tackle this slogan 'I like to start the day with Crispy Cornflakes because' in not more than ten words?"

"Don't ask me," retorted Tom, "Sunny and me have got better things to do than waste time on silly competitions."

"He might just as well be back at work for all I see of him"

Sunday

1

All Fools' Day
Palm Sunday

Monday

2

Tuesday

3

Wednesday

4

Thursday

5

Maundy Thursday

Friday

6

Good Friday (Bank Holiday)

Saturday

7

Oxford/Cambridge Boat Race

Sunday

8

Easter Sunday

Monday

9

Easter Monday (Bank Holiday, except Scotland)

Tuesday

10

Wednesday

11

Thursday

12

Friday

13

Saturday

14

The Grand National (Aintree)

Sunday

15

Monday

16

Tuesday

17

Wednesday

18

Thursday

19

Friday

20

Saturday

21

Queen's Birthday

Sunday

22

Flora London Marathon

Monday **23** <div align="right">**St George's Day**</div>	Friday **27**
Tuesday **24**	Saturday **28**
Wednesday **25**	Sunday **29**
Thursday **26**	Monday **30**

These hands of mine

Sometimes I wish for smaller hands,
Smooth and soft and pale.
Hands to flatter rings and things,
With never a ragged nail.

The kind of hands a man will take
And cherish in his own,
To make him feel protective
And keep me from being alone.

Such thoughts make me a traitor.
What foolishness is this?
For don't these hands of mine deserve
High praise for their true service?

Hard work throughout my life
Has left them gnarled and worn,
So I will treat them with respect
And never more will scorn!

Mrs Liz Richards, Malvern, Worcs

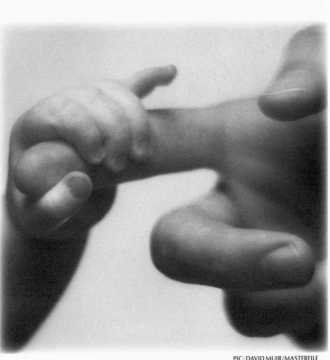

PIC: DAVID MUIR/MASTERFILE

Top Tip

To remove candle grease from fabric, just place brown paper over the top and iron over with a warm iron.

Winnie Sandham, Newquay

Your April health

Boost your energy levels for spring by starting your day with a shower using zingy grapefruit essential oil. Fill an egg cup with a plain oil, like sweet almond oil or even the sunflower oil you use for cooking. Add 12 drops of grapefruit essential oil (from health stores) and before you shower, massage the blend thoroughly into your abdomen. Then shower off, enjoying the refreshing citrus scent!

Healthy herbs

Chives

One of the easiest herbs to grow, chives are a relative of the onion, producing clumps of green leaves about 30cm in height with pretty light purple flowers. Chives are hardy and spread quickly, so lift and divide the plants when crowded. You can also collect the seeds and sow during spring. Cut fresh leaves as required – they'll add a subtle, onion-like taste. Grow them in your borders with other herbaceous perennials for a cottage garden feel.
Botanical name – *Allium schoenoprasum*
■ **Tip:** Cut up a few leaves and sprinkle them over your cheese on toast!

Top of the hit parade!

2 Apr 1964:
The Beatles
Can't Buy Me Love

4 Apr 1970:
Simon & Garfunkel
Bridge Over Troubled Water
(2nd week)

6 Apr 1974:
Terry Jacks
Seasons In The Sun

That special song

The song that brings back memories for me is Saturday Night At The Movies by The Drifters, not because it was one of my favourites but it was one of the tunes to which my small daughter practised her ballroom dancing. These sessions were at a local hall and she went on to win lots of medals. This tune was played continuously – and I used to wonder if it was because the teacher only had a small record collection!

As many of us mums didn't have the time to go home and come back for our girls, we often stayed at the hall and could have cheerfully broken the record by the end of the lesson! I'm sure it must have worn out eventually with all that constant playing.

Ballroom now seems to have had a new lease of life on the television so, who knows, I may hear '*that*' tune being played yet again – it's certainly memorable, but for all the wrong reasons!

Pat Rolfe, Hornchurch, Essex

Grace on the arm of her dad, Thomas Roberts, in 1960

Recipe of the week

Toffee Topped Rich Chocolate Pots

(Serves 6)

- 600 ml (1 pint) double cream
- 200 g (7 oz) plain chocolate (at least 60 per cent cocoa solids) chopped
- 1 teaspoon vanilla extract
- 225 g (8 oz) Billington's Unrefined Golden Caster sugar
- 3 tablespoons water

1 Heat the cream to boiling point in a large pan and remove from the heat. Pour the hot cream onto the chopped chocolate, a little at a time, mixing well until smooth.

2 Pour into 6 ramekins and chill for at least 3 hours. Heat the sugar and water in a pan over a low heat until the sugar has dissolved completely. Increase the heat until the mixture becomes a bubbling caramel – do not stir or the sugar will crystallise. Alternatively microwave the sugar and water to a bubbling golden caramel. It will take about 2 minutes – but watch it carefully as the time will depend on the size of container and the wattage of your microwave.

3 Remove from the heat immediately and allow the air bubbles to subside. Carefully spoon over the chilled chocolate mixture. The toffee will set at once.

RECIPE COURTESY BILLINGTON'S

My Dad

I was almost two years old when my Dad, Thomas, came home from the war in 1941. My first memory of him was of running down the street, forcing my little legs to run very fast and throwing myself into his outstretched arms.

He was unwell for the rest of his life and when I was married, in 1960, there was no question of him being able to buy my wedding dress. He had a little bit of pocket money each week and said that if I bought it, he would pay me back at 2/6d a week.

Fortunately, my friend's sister was selling hers; it was a flock nylon, ballerina length dress which fitted perfectly. She wanted £15 for it, but I hadn't the heart to tell my Dad, so I told him it was £10. Bless him, he spent the next couple of years paying the half-a-crown a week but he was so proud to say that he'd bought his daughter's dress.

Grace Brown, Oxford

Well I never...

The Royal Mail uses 342 million rubber bands a year to bundle up letters. They are usually red.

Well I never…

The wildlife documentary, March of the Penguins, was made for less than £4.5m but grossed more than £37m at the US box office.

Recipe of the week

Watercress and Salmon Soup
(Serves 4)

- 15 ml (1 tablespoon) sunflower oil
- 1 large onion, finely chopped
- 350 g (12 oz) potatoes, peeled and cut into rough cubes
- 1.5 litres (approx 2½ pints) vegetable stock or water
- 225 g (8 oz) watercress, roughly chopped
- 3 tablespoons single cream or reduced fat crème fraîche
- 175 g (6 oz) salmon, skinned and cut into cubes
- Salt and ground black pepper

1 Heat the oil in a large saucepan and add the onions and potatoes. Cook gently for 10 minutes until softened.
2 Add the stock or water and bring to the boil. Turn the heat down and simmer for 20 minutes. Stir in the watercress and cook for a further 5 minutes. Let the soup cool a little before liquidising it in batches. Return the soup to the pan and stir in the cream or crème fraîche. Taste and season with salt and ground black pepper.
3 When you are ready to serve the soup heat it to a low simmer. Add the salmon cubes and gently simmer for 5 minutes.

RECIPE COURTESY THE FRESH CUT STIR FRY ALLIANCE

Healthy herbs

Coriander

A hardy annual, coriander has finely-divided leaves and white flowers. The leaves have an earthy taste and the aromatic seeds, a rather mild orange-like flavour. Use the fresh growth – that produced before flowering has occurred – in your cooking and gather seeds as they ripen in summer. It's easily grown from seed sown during the spring. Botanical name – *Coriandrum sativum*

■ **Tip:** If you're not feeling peckish, add a few of the larger leaves at the end of cooking – coriander can be used medicinally as an appetite stimulant.

Top Tip

Reduce the fat content when frying food by decanting oil into a spray bottle to give a fine mist that doesn't saturate the food.

N Bourne, Sutton Coldfield

My Dad

Corinne with her Mum and Dad, Arthur and Mabel

Arthur, my Dad, always used to show me the scar just at the bottom of his ribs. He told me he got it while fighting in the First World War, when a bullet entered just below his ribs, and exited through his back. I was so fascinated to think that my Dad was such a hero.

When he died, aged 79, a very old friend of his came to the funeral. I remarked how lucky we were to have him all those years considering the narrow escape from death he had had during combat all those years before.

His friend then told me that my Dad never served in the war; he was exempt through medical reasons. Apparently, as a young boy he had pleurisy and because of the poverty and conditions at the time, the old doctor saved his life by operating on him, on the kitchen table, to drain the fluid from his lungs – hence the scar.

I still think the true explanation was just as dramatic as the fabricated one.

Mrs Corinne Beard, Plymouth

Meet my pet

This is Meg, our two-year-old bearded collie. When we went to choose a puppy from the litter, she was the smallest, prettiest and least outgoing of them all.

While her brothers and sisters were boisterously jumping around our legs, Meg set herself apart with a woeful expression on her face. Who could resist that? We certainly couldn't and have never regretted our decision – she is a most delightful dog who gives us endless pleasure.

Even passers-by think she's irresistible and they just have to stop and stroke her. Luckily, being retired, I'm able to devote as much time as I want to play with her, and in return she gives me love and companionship. Who could want more?

Margaret Jesson, Bridgnorth

Meg sitting waiting to play ball

Top of the hit parade!

11 Apr 1963:
Gerry & The Pacemakers
How Do You Do It?

13 Apr 1967:
Frank Sinatra & Nancy Sinatra
Somethin' Stupid

10 Apr 1968:
Cliff Richard
Congratulations

That special song

Dear Diary

March 19, 1987

This was such a special day for me, and this was my diary entry for the event:

'Sarah Louise was born. What a wonderful day – our first grandchild. Longing to see her! What a lucky girl to have been born to super parents. I pray for their joy and happiness always'.

Sarah will be 20 on March 19 and is a lovely grandchild of whom we are very proud.

Mary Smallwood, Leamington Spa

Our favourite song was I Haven't Said Thanks For That Lovely Weekend. My husband and I had become engaged in 1939 when I was only 19 but, having had our parents' permission, we married on November 11 that year.

Six weeks after this, my husband was called up to the Royal Engineers and was in the Army for six years. His leave was very precious to us and that song became our favourite.

After 61 years together, my husband died in 2001, but the happy memories still live on and the song is a reminder of those wonderful times.

Olive Salt, Buxton, Derbys

Olive with her great-grandson, Alexander

Sarah Louise, nearly a year old in 1988 and, below, Sarah today

Well I never...

It is said that the only occasion after the Second World War that Parisian traffic came to a complete standstill was for the funeral of Edith Piaf.

Healthy herbs

Horseradish

Although a native of Asia, this herb has naturalised in many countries including the UK. It's used extensively in cooking – the root can be grated fresh and used in horseradish sauce. If you want the strongest-tasting roots, then harvest them in autumn but remember that once cooked, the taste declines. A hardy perennial, horseradish reaches 90cm in height, and has insignificant flowers.
Botanical name – *Armoracia rusticana*
■**Tip:** Use horseradish as a companion plant with your root crops – it may help increase their disease resistance.

Recipe of the week

French Toast Sandwich with Peaches & Cream Cheese

(Serves 1)

- 2 slices fresh white bread
- 1 tablespoon low fat cream cheese
- 8 peach slices, fresh or tinned
- 1 egg, whisked
- 25 g (1 oz) butter
- Pinch of Tate & Lyle caster sugar
- Lyle's Golden Syrup Maple Flavour, to drizzle

1 Spread the slices of bread with cream cheese. Lay the peach slices onto one slice of bread and sandwich together with the other.
2 Dip both sides of the sandwich in the whisked egg.
3 Heat a frying pan. Pan fry in the butter till crisp and golden.
4 Remove from the pan and sprinkle with caster sugar. Slice in half and drizzle with Lyle's Golden Syrup Maple Flavour to serve.

RECIPE COURTESY TATE & LYLE

Top Tip

If you have problems with arthritic or weak hands, use a saucepan rather than a bowl when mixing to help control the movement.

Enid Dunscombe, Cardiff

Top of the hit parade!

16 Apr 1954:
Doris Day
Secret Love

22 Apr 1965:
Beatles
Ticket To Ride

16 Apr 1969:
Desmond Dekker & The Aces
Israelites

My Dad

'Your Dad is a very fine man'. I lost count of the number of times people said that to me when I was growing up in Ireland in the 1950s. I didn't appreciate what an extraordinary man he was until years later, for he became a widower at a young age and then I realised what a great sacrifice he made for me and my sisters and brother.

He had a full-time job as a train driver and worked shifts – I don't know how he managed to cope with it all, but he did. The rock and roll era couldn't have made life any easier for him. We three girls used to learn the jive in the kitchen when Dad had gone to bed. All we had was an old radio, which we turned down low, but if it disturbed Dad, he never complained.

We all emigrated to England and Dad joined us at the age of 72, and he lived to be 86. One day when we passed a community centre, a notice

Christina's Dad, Henry – 'a very fine man'

in the window said, 'Senior Citizens, come and join us'. I said to Dad: "Why don't you go, you might enjoy it." He looked at me, dumbfounded, and said: "Are you joking – that's for old people!"

Christina Kelly, Worcester

Well I never…

There are an estimated 200,000 people in the UK who have lost some or all of their sense of smell, the condition name being *anosmia*.

Recipe of the week

Chinese Pork

(Serves 4-6)

- 900 g (2 lb) lean boneless pork leg joint
- 5 ml (1 teaspoon) Chinese five spice
- 30 ml (2 tablespoons) brown sugar
- 30 ml (2 tablespoons) dark soy sauce
- 2 star anise
- 30 ml (2 tablespoons) Chinese cooking wine or sherry
- 2 garlic cloves, crushed
- 2.5 cm (1 in) root ginger, peeled and thinly sliced
- 200 ml carton pineapple juice

1 Cut the strings round the pork leg joint, flatten it out and place into a large ovenproof casserole dish.
2 Mix together the Chinese five spice, brown sugar, soy sauce, star anise, wine or sherry, garlic, root ginger. Add the pork, turn to coat in the marinade, cover and marinate in the fridge for about 30-60 minutes.
3 Add the pineapple juice, cover with a lid and cook for approximately 2 hours until meat is very tender. (Remove lid for the last 20 minutes to crisp outside).
4 Serve chunks or thick slices of the pork in a bowl with thick noodles and garnish with thin sticks of cucumber, spring onion and extra root ginger and a large spoonful of the juice.

RECIPE COURTESY BRITISH MEAT

Healthy herbs

Dill

A good herb if you suffer with wind, dill is a hardy annual with bluish-green stems, finely divided leaves and yellowish flowers. It's an active ingredient in gripe water and a tea made from a teaspoon of its seeds will cure dyspepsis, wind and stomach ache in adults.

Dill may reach 90cm in height, but is best cut back when around 30cm – the leaves can be used fresh or dry. Harvest the seeds when they're brown in colour. Both are used as a flavouring especially in pickles. Botanical name – *Anethum graveolens*

■ **Tip:** Dill can be invasive, so check all the seedheads are removed to prevent it popping up everywhere!

Top Tip

When rubber gloves have holes in the fingers, cut the wrists off to make rubber bands.
Brenda Griffiths, Rugby

My Dad

My dearest dad was W G – Billy – Richardson, the West Bromwich Albion and England footballer – and one of my memories of him is two years older than I am – he scored the two goals that beat Birmingham in the 1931 Cup Final at Wembley.

When I was little, every Saturday he would stroke my curls, kiss my forehead and say, 'Off to Arsenal' (or Liverpool or Manchester) and I hadn't got a clue where he was going, except I liked it when he went to Everton, because there would be a tin of Everton toffee on Sunday morning!

When he met Queen Juliana of the Netherlands, he came home with a pair of Dutch clogs for me and beautiful linen for Mum, and from a visit to Russia, he brought back a set of dolls – what a childhood, the daughter of W G Richardson. Sheer bliss!

Now here I am at 73 remembering how we lived like lords on his weekly wage of £18 and how we wonder at the thousands of pounds professional footballers earn today.

Even now I still meet people who talk about him with pride, having lost him at the age of 49 playing for the Showbiz Eleven team. *Moira Round, Birmingham*

Above: Billy and Moira's Mum kicking off a match at Ledbury in 1932
Left: Billy taking a limbering session by the West Brom players in 1949

Meet my pet

Elvis certainly seems at home on the sofa!

We found Elvis, our ginger tom, on the doorstep. He was half-starved and so weak he could hardly walk. His fur was matted and you could feel every bone in his little body.

He was terrified of people and noise, so we put food on the step for him at first. Gradually he became confident enough to come in but never stayed long. After about six months he decided to adopt us.

We took him to the vet, who told us he was deaf and blind on one side – for a cat that's almost certainly been due to illtreatment. However, he's a very cuddlesome cat.
Elaine Armer, Huddersfield

Top of the hit parade!

24 Apr 1959:
Buddy Holly
It Doesn't Matter Anymore

27 Apr 1967:
Sandie Shaw
Puppet On A String

24 Apr 1968:
Louis Armstrong
What A Wonderful World

On location at Alnwick Castle

History and Hogwarts

Alnwick Castle is the second largest inhabited castle in England after Windsor Castle. It is still the home of the Percy family who have been Earls and Dukes of Northumberland since 1309. Its beautiful grounds and adjacent Hulne Park have been the setting for many film and TV productions. As well as portraying the exterior of Hogwarts in the Harry Potter films, the castle has appeared in Becket (starring Peter O'Toole and Richard Burton) and Elizabeth (starring Cate Blanchett and Joseph Fiennes).

Built to defend England's northern border against the Scottish invasions, the castle consists of two rings. The inner ring is set around a small courtyard and contains the principal rooms. Special exhibitions are housed in three of the castle's perimeter towers. Visitors with an interest in archaeology will head for the Postern Tower to see frescoes from Pompeii, ancient Egyptian relics and Romano-British objects. Military memorabilia is housed in Constable's Tower, while the Abbot's Tower is the regimental museum of the Royal Northumberland Fusiliers.

The first Duke of Northumberland employed the celebrated architect Robert Adam to carry out restorations on the castle. Adam's work can still be seen in the fine ceilings and fireplaces and many of the stone figures guarding the battlements.

In the nineteenth century, the interior of Alnwick was opulently refurbished in the classical Italian Renaissance style.

The present Duchess of Northumberland has created an exciting contemporary garden that was officially opened in October 2002 by the Prince of Wales. The garden features a spectacular water display – known as the Grand Cascade – as well as a beautiful rose garden and one of the largest tree houses in the world.

Alnwick Castle is open from April through to the end of October.

■ *For further information, phone 01665 510777 or visit the website www.alnwickcastle.com*

Remember when…
Screen kiss

Anne Harvey of Chesterfield was an ardent picturegoer

In the 1950s, when I was in my early teens, I was a real film fan and spent all my money on magazines such as Picturegoer and Picture Show as well as going to the pictures. I read all about the stars and their activities, which were innocent enough back then!

I could afford to go to the pictures often because it was cheap; about 10d (3p) in the wooden seats at the very front, 1s 6d (15p) in the rear stalls. Although the films were usually a year or two out of date, the shows changed frequently with three films a week being shown.

My all-time favourite was Marlon Brando and I went to see On The Waterfront three times in one week. I never missed any film that Tony Curtis was in. Dirk Bogarde was one of my early heart-throbs and many years later I met him at a book signing in Leeds.

Our small Lancashire mill town was blessed with three cinemas. There was the posh one, called the Picture House. The less posh one had a tin roof which

Anne (right) in 1957 – cinema-going had plenty to offer

meant you couldn't hear the film when it rained. Once, when I went to the toilet, a cheeky mouse ran between my legs and shot under the door!

The real 'flea pit' was a tiny cinema called Johnny's. Saturday night at Johnny's was a real meeting place for the young people of the town. There was no chance of actually seeing or hearing the film – the cinema was too noisy with girls and boys chattering and swapping seats to be near each other. I had my very first kiss there – in the back row, of course!

Sport and History Quiz

Test your knowledge with these tricky teasers – if you get stuck the answers are at the bottom of the page.

PIC: REX FEATURES

1 Who was the third wife of Henry VIII?
a) Catherine of Aragon
b) Jane Seymour
c) Catherine Parr
d) Anne Boleyn

2 Roger Bannister broke the 4 minute mile in which year?
a) 1954
b) 1955
c) 1956
d) 1957

3 When did William Shakespeare die?
a) 1610
b) 1616
c) 1620
d) 1624?

4 Which classic horse race saw suffragette Emily Davison die under the hooves of the King's horse?
a) The Grand National
b) Cheltenham Gold Cup
c) Royal Ascot
d) The Epsom Derby

5 In which year was St George executed by beheading?
a) 303 AD
b) 528 AD
c) 127 AD
d) 96 BC

6 Who was the first manager of the England Football team?
a) Don Revie
b) Sir Alf Ramsey
c) Joe Mercer
d) Sir Walter Winterbottom

7 Which English King was popularly known as "Longshanks"?
a) Henry III
b) Edward I
a) Edward II
b) Richard III

8 Who has won the most Ladies Singles Championships at Wimbledon?
a) Billie Jean King
b) Steffi Graf
c) Martina Navrátilová
d) Venus Williams

9 When did Edward VIII (above) abdicate?
a) December 11, 1936
b) November 12, 1937
c) October 18, 1935
d) September 6, 1938

10 Which of these teams appeared in the 1986 FIFA World Cup but failed to score a goal?
a) USSR
b) Poland
c) Hungary
d) Canada

A New Grandma
by Sally Jenkins

How can Eunice win the hearts of two children who still miss their grandmother?

"That television is too loud, Jack." Eunice reached over to turn down the volume, feeling like the world's wickedest step-grandmother. "I can't hear it now," moaned the disconsolate six year old.

"I'm bored," whinged his older sister, Hannah. "I wish we had the computer to play on."

Eunice sighed. This seaside holiday with Sam and his grandchildren was proving hard work. Especially today when Sam had gone on a fishing trip, leaving her alone with them.

"Grandma used to take us to the ice-cream parlour when Granddad went fishing," hinted Hannah.

"It's a bit too close to lunchtime for that," said Eunice, "Why don't we have a walk along the beach and then I'll make us something to eat?"

"Do we have to?" said Jack.

"Yes," Eunice replied firmly and switched the television off.

"What about ice-cream?" asked Hannah.

"Maybe when Granddad gets back." Eunice hoped Sam wouldn't be late. She wished she were back at her office desk with a pile of orders to key into the computer. What a waste of a week's annual leave this was turning out to be.

The children complained bitterly when it started to drizzle as soon as they'd left the caravan park.

"Grandma gave us money for the amusement arcade when it rained," Hannah suggested helpfully.

"A bit of rain never hurt anyone," Eunice said briskly, thinking, 'I sound like my own grandmother, now'.

The beach was empty except for a few determined dog-walkers. Jack put his hood up against the sharp wind. Hannah poked pebbles out of the sand with her toe.

"Come on you two, the faster we walk, the warmer we'll get." Eunice waited for Jack to draw level with her.

"Grandma never hurried us," he said, adding in a whisper, "I wish she hadn't died."

Eunice felt as though someone had slapped her. Sam never spoke about his late wife and his grown-up children had accepted Eunice into their lives with warmth.

"Mark Carter's grandma died but his granddad didn't get a new wife." Eunice heard the resentment in the boy's voice.

"I'm not trying to take your grandma's place, Jack." She fumbled for the right words and gave up.

"Grandma played dominoes with us and taught us how to play patience."

"Your grandma sounds like a very clever lady."

"She was, but nobody talks about her now." Jack kept his eyes on his feet.

Eunice glanced up and realised his sister was no longer with them. "Where's Hannah?"

"Mum always changes the subject, too," grumbled Jack. "Whenever I mention grandma, she talks about something else."

Eunice's eyes swept frantically up and down the beach, searching for a blue denim jacket. An icy fear ran through her and newspaper headlines jumped into her brain: 'Nine year old lost on sand dunes', 'Girl's body washed up on beach'.

"She's down by the sea." Jack pointed to a distant figure throwing pebbles into the waves.

Grasping Jack's hand, Eunice hurried down to Hannah.

"Don't wander off like that again!" She struggled to stop herself shouting at the sulky looking girl. "Anything could have happened to you."

They continued along the beach in an uncomfortable silence. Jack broke into a trot at intervals to keep up with Eunice. She fingered the mobile phone in her pocket, tempted to call Sam to come back early and rescue her from these unhappy, bored children.

"I'm not trying to take your grandma's place, Jack"

"Look at that cat!" shouted Jack suddenly.

He was running across the sand to where a black-and-white cat appeared to be dragging itself along the waters edge. Eunice and Hannah hurried behind him.

"He's all wet," said the boy, stroking the animal's head.

The cat mewed plaintively.

"He's got string around his back legs," said Hannah, "That's why he can't walk properly."

Eunice bent down and tugged at the string which was embedded in the flesh of one leg. She straightened up and turned to the children: "I think someone tried to drown him."

"That's horrible," said Hannah in anguish. "We can't just leave him here. He'll die. Let's take him back to the caravan."

Eunice ran her hand tenderly along the emaciated body: "I think he needs to see a vet first."

Hannah tried to pick the cat up but it lashed out with one of its front paws, drawing blood. Shocked, she dropped the wet animal.

"Be careful!" shouted Jack, "Don't hurt him."

"My face is bleeding," Hannah gingerly felt her cheek.

Eunice handed her a clean handkerchief and then took off her own anorak, ignoring the chilly wind. "Here, wrap him in my jacket. With his paws covered up he can't hurt you."

Together they managed to secure the struggling cat and Hannah carried the swaddled animal close to her as they hurried off the beach. Jack kept reaching up to stroke the furry head protruding from the jacket.

"I'm sure we passed a vet's surgery near here," said Eunice. "Yes. There it is, over the road."

"This is one very lucky animal," said the vet as he cleaned the cat's wounds. "All he needs now is a good dinner and some TLC."

"I'll look after him!" Jack could hardly contain his excitement.

"Mum will never let us," said Hannah, gloomily. "She won't even let us have a goldfish."

Eunice took a deep breath – it was time to build bridges in this relationship. "Your granddad and I will have him and then you two can come and see him whenever you want."

Jack took hold of her hand and Hannah smiled cautiously.

'It's a start', thought Eunice.

Hannah tried to pick the cat up but it lashed out

May 2007

Tuesday

1

Wednesday

2

Thursday

3

Friday

4

Saturday

5

Royal May Day celebration

Sunday

6

Monday

7

May Day (Early May Bank Holiday)

Tuesday

8

Wednesday

9

Thursday

10

Friday

11

Saturday

12

Sunday

13

Monday

14

Tuesday

15

Wednesday

16

Thursday

17

Ascension Day

Friday

18

Saturday

19

Sunday

20

Monday

21

Tuesday

22

Chelsea Flower Show begins

Wednesday	Monday
23	**28**
	Spring Bank Holiday
Thursday	Tuesday
24	**29**
Friday	Wednesday
25	**30**
Saturday	Thursday
26	**31**
Sunday	
27	
Whit Sunday or Pentecost	

PIC: MASTERFILE

The Bluebell Wood

I came upon them quite by chance,
A lovely sight to see.
They made one think of Heaven
And all good things to be.

And as far as the eye could see
They stood up, tall and straight,
Just like the sentry by the Palace gate.
Bluer than the sky they were,

Bluer than the sea.
I knew someone had planted them
Especially for me.

And in my memory I still recall
The day I chanced that way,
And saw them in their glory
On that warm and sunny day.
Mrs M Day, Southampton, Hants

Dear Diary

May 3, 1935

The Silver Jubilee of King George V and Queen Mary

There is a Jubilee feeling in the air, the weather is sunny and warm and I've put on my black and white summer dress

They've been giving away balloons and flags at the shop. The Laundry Gardens (Derby) look lovely decorated with flags. Looks as though the weather is going to be kind to the King on his Jubilee.

May 5

Went with Ted and Bob on the motorbike in the afternoon. All the little villages in the Peak are covered with flags and there are beacons on the highest hills…

May 6

To Brackens Farm for the Jubilee sports – crowds of people there, Charlie came second in the slow bicycle race. PC was on duty with a beaming smile from ear to ear. Bonfire was lit, followed by fireworks.

Written by my mother, Kathleen Garratt when she was 19. The Police Constable mentioned became her husband in 1937.

Pamela Hulbert, Buxton, Derbyshire

Above: Pamela's Dad (right) with his Sergeant
Right: Pamela's Mum Kathleen (centre) on an excursion to Dove Dale in 1932

Healthy herbs
Fennel

Plant fennel in the centre of your border where you can enjoy its finely divided leaves - it provides a lovely textural element to a planting scheme and reaches 1.5m in height. Fennel grows easily from seed but may need staking in windy gardens. Harvest the seeds when they're ripe and use as a condiment – they have an aniseed-like taste. The tender flower stalks can be eaten like celery.
Botanical name – *Foeniculum vulgare*
■ **Tip:** An infusion of seeds can be used to cure colic and heartburn.

Top Tip

Crush chocolate Bourbon biscuits with a rolling pin and sprinkle over trifles etc, for a crunchy topping.   *M Jones, Eastbourne*

Your May health

Hay fever season is here, and you could already be experiencing wheezes and sneezes. Invest in wide sunglasses to stop pollens affecting your eyes, and wipe petroleum jelly around your nostrils to stop them getting up your nose. Keep windows shut when you can, and wash your hair whenever you come inside, to rinse the pollens out. The herb butterbur can help, too – ask in your local health food store. Visit www.allergyuk.org

Recipe of the week
Fresh Lemon Meringue Cake
(Serves 8-10)

For the cake
- 150 g (5 oz) plain flour
- 1 tablespoon baking powder
- Pinch of salt
- 110g (4 oz) unsalted butter
- 110g (4 oz) Billington's Unrefined Golden Caster Sugar
- Finely grated zest and juice of 3 lemons
- 4 egg yolks

For the meringue
- 4 egg whites
- Pinch of salt
- 110g (4 oz) Billington's Unrefined Golden Caster sugar

1 Sift the flour, baking powder and salt together.
2 Cream the butter, sugar and lemon zest until light and fluffy, then gradually beat in the egg yolks. Beat in the flour mixture a little at a time with the lemon juice until well blended.
3 Spoon into a greased, lined 24cm (9 inch) round cake tin. Whisk the egg whites and the salt until softly peaking, then gradually whisk in the sugar a little at a time, whisking continuously until the mixture is stiff and shiny. Spoon evenly over the cake mixture.
4 Place the tin on a low shelf in the oven as the meringue rises enormously as it cooks. Cook for about 40 minutes at 160°C, 310°F, Gas Mark 3 until the cake is cooked through and the meringue is crisp and golden.
5 Remove from the oven and cool in the tin. The meringue will sink and pull away from the sides of the cake as it cools.

RECIPE COURTESY BILLINGTON'S

Well I never…

'I believe that love cannot be bought except with love, and he who has a good wife wears heaven in his hat'.
From the film Viva Zapata

My Dad

I am 67 years old, but will never forget my wonderful Dad, even though I didn't know him for very long as he died when I was only nine. Sometimes my sister and I will talk about him and we'll have a good laugh.

He worked as a baker, so he had to get up at three or four in the morning. He almost always had toast for breakfast, and if I heard him get up or smelled his toast, I'd creep downstairs and he would save the crusts for me. It was a magical time as I got to see Dad for a little longer.

Eva Sandiford, Bury, Lancashire

Above: Eva's parents on their wedding day

Top of the hit parade!

5 May 1960:
Everly Brothers
Cathy's Clown

2 May 1963:
Beatles
From Me To You

5 May 1966:
Manfred Mann

Well I never…

Here are some names to conjure with:
Did you know that the singer Buffy Sainte-Marie called her child Dakota Star Blanket Wolfchild? Or that Smokey Robinson's children are called Tamla and Berry?

Recipe of the week
Trout Wrapped with Parma Ham and Spinach Lentils

(Serves 4)
- 4 trout fillets, skinless, weighing about 175 g (6 oz)
- Salt and ground black pepper
- 8 slices of Parma ham
- Olive oil
- 400 g (1 lb) can lentils
- Juice of 1 lemon
- Handful parsley and coriander, roughly chopped
- 100 g (4 oz) spinach, roughly chopped
- 1 small red onion, finely chopped
- 1 garlic clove, crushed

1 Season the trout fillets with a little pepper and roll up, wrap each fillet in two Parma ham slices.
2 Drizzle with olive oil and roast in the oven at around 220°C, 425°F, or Gas Mark 7 for around 10 minutes or until the Parma ham is golden.
3 Drain the lentils and season with salt, pepper, lemon juice and 4 tbsp olive oil. Just before serving, add the herbs and spinach and stir over a high heat until the spinach begins to wilt.
4 Add the red onion and garlic and season well. Serve the trout on a spoonful of lentils.

RECIPE COURTESY THE BRITISH TROUT ASSOCIATION

Healthy herbs

Hyssop

A lovely Mediterranean herb, hyssop is woody with small pointed leaves and spires of purple, pink or white flowers. Plant in a sunny, well-drained soil or sow seed during spring. It thrives in poor conditions and makes a pleasing, if short-lived, hedge. Use the youngest leaves sparingly, and the flowers, in green salads – they have a sweet aniseed-like taste.
Botanical name – *Hyssopus officinalis*
- **Tip:** Hyssop will attract pollinating insects into the garden.

Top Tip

To keep string tidy, store it in a funnel hung on the wall and draw the string through the hole.
K Croft, Hayling Island

Top of the hit parade!

13 May 1955:
Tony Bennett
Stranger In Paradise

15 May 1959:
Elvis Presley
A Fool Such As I

13 May 1965:
Roger Miller
King Of The Road

My Dad

As one of 13 children and with a widowed mother, my Dad, Harold, left school and went to work with some of his brothers down the pit at Farnley in Leeds. He worked up to his waist in water all day – and there were no pit baths or showers after work then. He endured these conditions for many years until he left the job on medical advice.

My Mum died, aged 25, leaving my Dad a widower at 29. We lived with my Grandmother because Dad had to keep working, to 'keep the cart on the wheels'. He never remarried, so I suppose looking back he must have been lonely.

I can still remember him putting me to bed every night and laying at the side of me while singing me to

Kathleen's Dad, Harold, mending the gate, around 1953

sleep with songs such as Nellie Dean and If Those Lips Could Only Speak.

He was a kind, happy man in spite of a sometimes miserable life. How I still love and admire him.

Kathleen Wright, Tadcaster

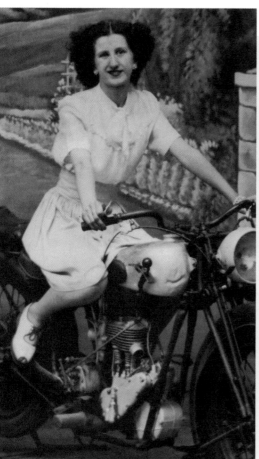

That special song

The song that stands out for me is People Will Say We're In Love from Oklahoma! I believe the year was 1947 when the show was at its height in London

My friend and I were on holiday in Blackpool with my Mother and Father, and dancing being our forte, the song was played all the time, along with all the hits from the show.

Life was wonderful in Blackpool that year for a couple of 16 year olds just blossoming out from our school days, into what we thought were wasp-waist wenches with lots of pulling power. Donned in our dirndle skirts of powder blue that Mother made for us, life was wonderful in Blackpool that year.

I have been a member of Nuneaton Amateur Society for 25 years and Oklahoma! was performed many times – and every time Carrie and Curley sang 'that' duet, I was transported back to that magical holiday at Blackpool in 1947.

I'm now 75 and the memory of dancing in the Tower Ballroom to Reg Dixon's organ music and, at the end of the pier, to this lovely song will always stay with me.

Olive Byhurst, Bedworth

Olive at the pleasure beach,
having her photo taken on a motorbike

Top Tip

If a disabled person finds it difficult getting in and out of the car, place a plastic carrier bag on the seat and they'll find it easier to swivel round.

C Beard, Plymouth

Meet my pet

My late, little feathered friend – Jackie – was such a good companion to me.

He liked a drink of beer, and after a few sips he could lisp his way through I Belong to Glasgow. Jackie could also give you his address – I do miss my lovely friend.

Mrs Iris Barter, Sherborne

Left: Jackie enjoying his tipple

Top of the hit parade!

18 May 1961:
Floyd Kramer
On The Rebound

20 May 1965:
Jackie Trent
Where Are You Now (My Love)

18 May 1967:
Tremeloes
Silence Is Golden

Healthy herbs
Lavender

Everyone loves lavender – it has such an amazing scent. It also has many uses around the home. A woody perennial, lavender may reach between 30 and 90cm in height with silvery leaves and purple, blue and almost-red flowers during summer, depending on variety. It loves well-drained soils and plenty of sunshine and can be propagated by seed or cuttings. Harvest the whole flower stem just as it's starting to open, then hang in bunches to dry. Use the flowers in sachets to scent rooms, drawers and airing cupboards, as a flavouring when making cakes and use lavender oil to treat burns, stings and cuts.
Botanical name – *Lavandula angustifolia*
■ **Tip:** A pretty garden plant, place a few leaves under your pillow to help you sleep or, during the summer, use it as an insect repellent.

Well I never…

The original FA Cup was stolen from a sports shop in Birmingham in 1895 and was never returned.

Recipe of the week

Banana Bran Muffins

(Makes: 12)

- 75 g (3 oz) unsalted butter
- 3 ripe medium bananas
- 2 medium eggs
- 240 ml (8 fl oz) semi-skimmed milk
- 200 g (7 oz) plain flour
- 2 tsps baking powder
- 75 g (3 oz) Tate & Lyle Light Soft Light Brown Sugar
- 1 tsp ground cinnamon
- 25 g (1 oz) bran (cereal bran)

1 Preheat oven to 190°C, 375°F, or Gas 5. Line a 12-hole muffin tin with paper muffin cases.
2 Melt the butter in a small pan over a moderate heat or in a microwave.
3 In a medium bowl mash the bananas using a fork and add the eggs, milk and melted butter and stir together.
4 Sift the flour, baking powder, sugar and cinnamon together into another bowl and stir in the bran. Tip the dry ingredients into the wet ingredients and gently fold together.
5 Spoon the mixture into the cases, filling them three-quarters full. Bake in the middle of the oven for 15-20 minutes or until they have turned golden-brown in colour.
6 Remove the muffins from the tin and allow to cool on a wire rack.

RECIPE COURTESY TATE & LYLE

My Dad

My Dad, Walter, worked as a steam roller driver for West Riding County Council but he wanted me to go to college and get a better job. He worked all the overtime he could get, mending roads in the summer and gritting in the winter.

In his spare time he loved his garden, growing flowers in the front and neat rows of vegetables in the back. He also had a small piece of land next to our bungalow where he kept hens.

He was not at all demonstrative but on the day I left home to go to college he and Mum went with me to Leeds, to see me off on the train, and I was amazed to see tears in his eyes.

When I qualified as a teacher, I went home to live and teach in the local school. However, when I went to the cinema I never saw the end of a film until I was married, as I had to be back in good time. He believed that even though I now earned more than him, while I lived in his house, I followed his rules. And I did.

Barbara Cox, Hexham, Northumberland

Above: Barbara's parents, Walter and Ethel in 1967
Below: Little Barbara, with her Mum and dad in 1940

Dear Diary

Saturday, May 19, 1934

'Had the afternoon off and walked over the fields to Elvaston Church. We waited in the church yard and when they carried the coffin in, I daren't look at first, but looked at the white stone angel with the fir trees rustling behind it'.

The young diarist was my 18-year-old mother and the funeral was of her grandfather, Robert Garratt, stonemason to Lord Harrington at Elvaston Castle.

One of his last tasks had been to put up this beautiful angel over the Harrington vault. It watched over the churchyard and five generations of my ancestors until vandals toppled it over in recent years. A sad reflection on our times.

Pamela Hulbert, Buxton, Derbyshire

Above: Robert Garratt with his mother, son and grandson in 1913
Right: Pamela's Mum, Kathleen, who wrote the diary
Above, right: The Harrington Angel, Elvaston Church, 1953

John Albert outside his garage in 1959

My Dad

John Albert Young, my Dad, was born in 1892, the eldest of a family of six. Having been a porter, he then worked for himself, making deliveries in his lorry all over London.

Dad would go out early and load up, then come in for his breakfast before he started off – and in the summer holidays, I would go with him. After he got the signal from the policeman on point duty to 'go ahead', he'd always bang on the outside of his driving door and shout, 'Crabby copper!' – I was scared stiff he'd get into trouble.

Dad later had his own garage, and this photo of him is one of my favourites. I always said he could go to Buckingham Palace in his working clothes and not feel out of place! He died in 1976, aged 84.

Queenie M Edkins, Ware, Herts

That special song

Dorothy and her late husband, John

My late husband, John, and my special song was (and is) True Love from High Society. He started to sing the song on our honeymoon, and always after that it was our very special song – we really did have a true love.

Dorothy Burder, Bury St Edmunds, Suffolk

Top Tip

Wash and dry a used freezer bag and pop a potted seed pot in and seal, opening up when they appear to give your seeds an early start.

J Webb, Swindon

Healthy herbs

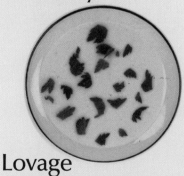

Lovage

Rather unsurprisingly considering its name, lovage was used as an aphrodisiac in the sixteenth century. A hardy perennial, it has large leaves that resemble those of celery – they also taste similar, but are stronger and sweeter, so can be used to spice up soups and salads. The seeds can be added to bread mixtures. Plant lovage in a moist soil in sun or partial shade and feed regularly during the growing season. Sow seeds during early summer.
Botanical name – *Levisticum officinale*
■ **Tip:** Cut back to encourage fresh young leaves as these are the best for cooking.

Top of the hit parade!

24 May 1962:
Elvis Presley
Good Luck Charm

27 May 1965:
Sandie Shaw
Long Live Love

26 May 1966:
Rolling Stones
Paint It Black

Recipe of the week

Asparagus, Bacon and Poached Egg Salad with a Mustard Dressing
(Serves 4)

For the dressing
- 6 tablespoons olive oil
- 2 tablespoons cider vinegar
- 2 teaspoons sugar
- 1 teaspoon Dijon mustard
- 2 teaspoons wholegrain mustard
- 2 cloves crushed garlic
- Sea salt & black pepper

For the salad
- 2 bundles British asparagus
- 4 teaspoons wine vinegar
- 4 eggs
- 4 generous handfuls mixed salad leaves
- 4 rashers smoked streaky bacon cut into small strips and cooked until crispy
- 2 tablespoons bread croutons

1 Combine the dressing ingredients and season to taste.
2 Clean the asparagus and trim any white ends or peel with a vegetable peeler.
3 Cook the asparagus in boiling, salted water for 3 minutes or until just tender, drain well and toss in a teaspoonful of dressing.
4 Meanwhile, bring a pan of salted water to the boil and add the wine vinegar. Turn the heat down to a simmer, crack the eggs and gently drop the contents into the water. Leave for approximately 3 minutes or until the white is set. Remove with a slotted spoon and drain.
5 Arrange a handful of salad leaves on each plate, top with warm asparagus, bacon and croutons and place a poached egg on top. Drizzle with dressing and a twist of black pepper.

RECIPE COURTESY WWW.BRITISH-ASPARAGUS.CO.UK

Well I never…

The London borough of Westminster has around 20 pieces of chewing gum for every square metre of pavement.

Meet my pet

We are puppy walkers for Guide Dogs for the Blind and our first four-footed 'customer', Jason, may look small in the photo, but he had a voracious appetite and would eat anything in his path.

On one occasion, Jason was caught in the act of scoffing some cat litter, so we contacted our supervisor and vet to see if there may be any dire effects. Thankfully, they thought he'd be okay.

The next day was a joy because, as we cleaned up Jason's 'deposits,' the deodorant in the litter sanitised all his offerings! We did jokingly ask the supervisor if we could make it a regular part of his diet but (for some reason) she didn't seem to think it a good idea!

Beverly Collins, Huddersfield

Left: Jason and his master. Such a little pup and such a large appetite!

Well I never...

'There are now more TVs in British households than there are people – which is a bit of a worry'.
Prince Charles

Top of the hit parade!

1 Jun 1961:
Elvis Presley
Surrender

28 May 1964:
Cilla Black
You're My World

2 Jun 1966:
Frank Sinatra
Strangers In The Night

Healthy herbs
Sweet marjoram

Sweet marjoram is one of the most fragrant herbs. Shrubby, it has a low and spreading habit and rarely reaches more than 30cm in height. Its small, oval, greyish leaves can be used all year round, fresh or dried, in cooking. It's only half-hardy, so overwinter it in a container indoors or sow seed every spring. You can also take cuttings.
Botanical name
– *Origanum majorana*
■ **Tip:** Plant it in the border during summer – it makes an attractive bedding plant.

Recipe of the week

Caramelised Caribbean Pineapple

Serves 4

- 25 g (1 oz) unsalted butter
- 1 pineapple, skinned and cubed
- Generous pinch of cinnamon
- Generous pinch of mixed spice
- 2 tablespoons Lyle's Squeezy Syrup, Toffee Flavour
- Vanilla ice cream, to serve

1 Pre-heat the oven to 190°C, 375°F, or Gas Mark 5.
2 Melt the butter gently in a medium-sized saucepan then remove from the heat. Add the Squeezy Syrup, cinnamon and mixed spice and stir to mix.
3 Toss the pineapple cubes in the mixture to coat, then spread them out on a tray and bake in the oven for 10-15 minutes until golden brown on the edges but still firm.
4 Remove from the oven and serve with the ice cream.

RECIPE COURTESY TATE & LYLE

My Dad

My Dad, William, was born in Hackney and was the youngest of four, his mum having died when he was 12. At 18, he was called up as a Lewis gunner in the First World War and saw action at Passchendaele.

He told me of the mud, the shell holes filled with water and, if you fell in, you were lucky if you managed to scramble out. Dad said how they were pushing towards enemy lines, when he and his mate, Ted, took cover in a recent shell hole – the fire coming over thick and fast. Ted had a feeling they needed to get out. Dad wanted to stay put but decided to go with his mate. Seconds later a shell landed where they'd been resting. Dad said he owed his life to Ted.

Being in the trenches gave Dad trench foot, so he was invalided out to hospital in England and, after weeks of treatment, was sent to an army camp in Norfolk.

He was told he'd been chosen to go to Sandringham to chauffeur King George V and Queen Mary for six weeks. Dad couldn't believe it, he'd come from a poor family in the East End and here he was, driving the King!

Dad said it was the best six weeks of his army life. He ate in the royal kitchens, went on shoots with the King (Dad said he was a good shot – six shots, six birds) but he let out a few choice words when he tripped getting into the car one day!

Olive Stone, Farnham, Surrey

Right: Olive with her Dad, William, 'Digging for Victory' during the Second World War

Places to visit

On location at Hatfield House

Queen Elizabeth slept here

Hatfield House became Greenwich Palace in the film Shakespeare in Love where Queen Elizabeth I (Dame Judi Dench) watched a firework display. The house was built in 1611 by Robert Cecil, 1st Earl of Salisbury and chief minister to King James I and has remained in the Cecil family ever since.

Superb examples of Jacobean craftsmanship can be seen throughout the house: the grand staircase boasts a wealth of intricate detail carved in wood and there is a rare stained glass window in the private chapel.

Close to the house is the surviving wing of the ancient Royal Palace of Hatfield where Elizabeth I spent much of her childhood. It was here that she held her first Council of State in 1558.

In Hatfield House itself, you can see many historic mementoes collected over the centuries by the Cecils, one of England's most distinguished political families. The third Marquess of Salisbury was three times Prime Minister during the reign of Queen Victoria. The sumptuously furnished state rooms on the first floor include the King James' drawing room, the library and a long gallery. The national collection of model soldiers can also be found at Hatfield.

The beautiful garden dates from the early seventeenth century when Robert Cecil employed John Tradescant the Elder to collect plants for his new home. A horticultural pioneer, Tradescant introduced trees, bulbs and plants that had never previously been grown in England. The garden was restored in the Victorian era by Lady Gwendolen Cecil who designed the West Garden as it is today. On Thursdays, all 42 acres of the garden, including the kitchen garden, are open to the public. Also in the grounds are a children's play area, a picnic site and five miles of marked trails for walkers.

■ *For further information, phone 01707 287010 or visit the website www.hatfield-house.co.uk.*

Remember when…
Wash and brush up

Bridget Hole of Maidenhead was in awe of Sister

I had tonsillitis and was admitted to Maidenhead cottage hospital as an emergency. As there was no room on the children's ward, I was put on a women's ward.

Two days after my operation, I was well enough to get up and go to the bathroom to wash. I was waiting outside for another patient to finish in the one bathroom that served the whole ward when I saw a nurse walking resolutely towards me. She was dressed in dark blue with an impressive belt and magnificent white lace cap. "Why are you standing there?" she demanded. I was so terrified, I just pointed at the closed door. "Come with me," she said sharply, moving off at a rate of knots. I thought I was going to be thrown out or reported to the police. After walking down what seemed like miles of corridors, this fearsome lady opened the door of the most opulent bathroom I had ever seen. At home we only had cold water and a Burco boiler to heat the water on bath days. This one had hot and cold water, fluffy towels and nice-smelling soap.

Saying: "Leave it as you find it," the nurse disappeared. I was so nervous that I merely dampened my flannel to wipe my face, polished the basin with my towel where water had splashed on it and furtively made my way

Bridget in 1950

back to the ward.

Many years later, my husband and I were pleased to make the acquaintance of the charming elderly couple who lived opposite. He had been a teacher and she had been a nurse. Yes, it was the same Sister who had shown such concern for me all those years ago and allowed me to use the bathroom reserved for private patients.

Lyrical Word Play

PIC: REX FEATURES

Can you work out the real titles of these famous Beatles songs from the rather literal translations given below? Don't worry if you get stuck – the answers are at the bottom of the page

1 Cry For Assistance

2 The Day Before Today

3 Control One's Vehicle

4 Scandinavian Forest

5 Non-Existent Male

6 During The Existence Belonging To Me

7 Collector Of Income Deductions

8 One Is Merely Dormant

9 Must Acquire And Position You Within My Being

10 Rosaceous Fruit Pasture Eternally

11 One Hundredth Of A Pound Passage

12 NCO Condiment's Forlorn Association Group

13 Female In The Atmosphere By Means Of Rhombus

14 After I Become Three Score Years Plus Four

15 24 Hours In The Existence

16 Supernatural Secrecy Trip

17 One Is The Tusked Aquatic Carnivore

18 Species Of Thrush

19 Fairground Spiral Slide

20 Approach Jointly

21 An Undefined Object

22 Now Approaches The Centre Of Our Planetary System

ANSWERS: 1 Help!, **2** Yesterday, **3** Drive My Car, **4** Norwegian Wood, **5** Nowhere Man, **6** In My Life, **7** Taxman, **8** I'm Only Sleeping, **9** Got To Get You Into My Life, **10** Strawberry Fields Forever, **11** Penny Lane, **12** Sgt. Pepper's Lonely Hearts Club Band, **13** Lucy In The Sky With Diamonds, **14** When I'm Sixty-Four, **15** A Day In The Life, **16** Magical Mystery Tour, **17** I Am The Walrus, **18** Blackbird, **19** Helter Skelter, **20** Come Together, **21** Something, **22** Here Comes The Sun

A hair-raising tale

Elizabeth McKay spent many a sleepless night with her hair in rollers, as her mum would never give in to her daughter's straight hair. Ouch!

My niece sent me a photograph the other day of her little girl's first school photograph. She looked very sweet in her uniform with her blonde hair hanging neatly in bunches and tied with purple ribbons.

Looking at the picture brought back memories of my own childhood in the 1960s and the dreaded preparations for the school photograph.

I've always had thick, straight hair but for some reason my mother always wanted it to look curly on special occasions such as Sunday School parties or school photographs. So on the day in question, out would come those 'instruments of torture', the curling tongs.

While the tongs were heating in the fire, I'd embark on some last minute negotiations. What if I promised to eat all my crusts every day for the rest of my life? Sadly, my bargaining powers weren't up to much and pretty soon I gave in and accepted my fate.

As soon as my mother deemed the tongs hot enough, she took them from the fire and wiped them with a sheet of newspaper to get rid of the soot and ashes. I braced myself while she applied the red hot instruments to a strand of my hair. There was a slight sizzling sound as contact was made and my nose twitched nervously as a faint whiff of something scorching hit my nostrils.

My mother would then start the curling process, gripping my hair between the metal prongs and rolling it up tightly towards my scalp. The tighter it got, the tenser I became, praying that she'd remember to stop before the tongs touched my head. Thankfully she always did.

The whole process – heating, wiping, rolling, praying – was repeated several times until my mother was satisfied with the result. Sadly, her hairdressing skills left a lot to be desired, and for the rest of the day I simply avoided looking in any mirrors. If it hadn't been for the photographic evidence a few weeks later, I might have been able to convince myself that I really did look like Shirley Temple.

I'm not sure what happened to the curling tongs. Perhaps, they were inadvertently thrown out during an over-enthusiastic bout of spring cleaning. I emphatically deny any knowledge of their disappearance.

However, my mother's ambitions for a daughter with curly hair were not about to be thwarted. Rollers were the answer.

First, she tried sponge rollers which wouldn't poke into me while I was sleeping. The trouble was my hair was too thick for them to grip properly and in the morning I'd wake up to find one solitary little pink tube of pink foam stoically hanging on to my fringe.

Desperate measures were required and there was nothing else for it but to move on to plastic rollers with tiny spikes to grip the hair and cages to hold them firmly in place.

One of my school friends wore her hair in ringlets. She used to complain that she had to go to bed each night with strips of cloth twisted around her hair. She should have tried getting a decent night's sleep with 20 or more spiked rollers jabbed all over her head.

By the time I reached my teens my hair was longer, straighter, and thicker than ever. My mother became resigned that curls were

Left: Elizabeth 'going straight'

Below, right: Torture by curling tongs

Below, left: That perm…

not for me. Besides she had other things to concern herself with – like the length of my skirts and what treatment I'd require when I fell off my inch high platform shoes.

But she did have one last stab at reviving the dream when on my 21st birthday she presented me with a set of Carmen heated rollers.

I went straight for several years. Until the eighties, in fact, when perms became all the rage for both men and women.

"I don't want it to look too curly," I said to the hairdresser, "just a nice, soft wave, to give my hair a bit of bounce."

She smiled, nodded and obviously didn't listen to a word I said. Two hours later I emerged from the salon looking like Harpo Marx's sister.

I cried for an entire weekend and didn't leave the house until I had to go to work on Monday morning.

My colleagues were sympathetic and assured me it would soon grow out. It did – sideways, making me look even more like a circus clown than ever. Needless to say my mother thought it looked lovely!

I had it chopped at the first opportunity and vowed never again. Short and thick- haired is what I am and that is the way I'll stay. As long as I have access to a hairdryer and a brush, I can't go far wrong.

Sometimes when I'm flicking through glossy magazines in the hairdresser's salon I come across a style that looks particularly tempting – wispy curls falling softly over the model's face, for instance – and I think maybe that would look okay on me.

Then I force myself to dredge up memories of that perm and I shudder. By the time the stylist asks me what I'd like doing today I simply shrug and say: "Just the usual, please."

Nowadays curls are the least of my worries. Every morning when I look in the mirror it seems like a hundred more grey hairs have sprouted up overnight.

To dye or not to dye – that is the question that has perplexed people of a certain age for many years. Should one simply give in and grow old gracefully? Or should you let your hair down and hit the bottle? The dye bottle, that is.

I mentioned this dilemma to a male friend the other day. He shrugged and tapped the top of his shiny head.

"Grey, purple, green, blue – who cares?" he sighed. "I just wish I had some to worry about."

Friday

1

Saturday

2
Anniversary of Elizabeth II's coronation

Sunday

3
Trinity Sunday

Monday

4

Tuesday

5

Wednesday

6
The Derby, Epsom

Thursday

7

Friday

8

Saturday

9
Trooping The Colour (Queen's official birthday)

Sunday

10

Monday

11

Tuesday

12

Wednesday

13

Thursday

14

Friday

15

Saturday

16

Sunday

17
Fathers' Day

Monday

18

Tuesday

19

Wednesday

20

Thursday

21
Summer solstice

Friday

22

Saturday 23	**Wednesday** 27
Sunday 24	**Thursday** 28
Monday 25 **Wimbledon Lawn Tennis Championship Begins**	**Friday** 29
Tuesday 26	**Saturday** 30 **Cheltenham Music Festival begins**

PIC: KEVIN DODGE/MASTERFILE

A Picnic

Out on a picnic, just we two,
And we know just what to do.
We park the car in some leafy glade,
Then eat the sarnies and tea we made.
Now is the time to have a doze,
So we both sit back in sweet repose,
The papers read and the books put away,
We sleep and dream: what a perfect day.

Mrs Eileen Nieser, Lancing, West Sussex

June 4-10

Jenny's Dad, Ted, catching up with the Sunday papers

Top of the hit parade!

7 Jun 1957:
Johnnie Ray
Yes Tonight Josephine

8 Jun 1967:
Procol Harum
A Whiter Shade Of Pale

4 Jun 1969:
Tommy Roe
Dizzy

My Dad

Ted with granddaughter Sophie

There are lots of wonderful memories about my Dad but I especially remember mornings when my sister and I would come downstairs to breakfast to find a cheery good morning note from him (already long gone off to work) in the hands of one of our favourite dolls, seated on the kitchen table beside our cereal bowls.

This would often be on days when something special might be happening such as a school outing, when he might leave sixpence spending money, or in the summer, when we were going to the beach, he'd write something such as, 'If you swallow sea water, be careful to spit out the fish!'.

He was a good DIY man, he devised board games and quiet things to do when we were ill and, as teenagers, he was always there in the background, ready to come to the rescue, fixing a broken handbag strap, or making small talk to a boyfriend.

And he came into his own with the grandchildren – how he loved them!

Jenny Jewiss, Eastbourne, East Sussex

Healthy herbs
Oregano

Oregano is also called wild marjoram but is much hardier than sweet marjoram. A perennial with sprawling stems, it's quite coarse in habit and smells more like thyme. It has small pink or white flowers and grows well in poor soils. Propagate by sowing seed in spring or dividing large plants. Use fresh leaves as required or dry them and use on pizza.
Botanical name – *Origanum vulgare*
■ **Tip:** Stimulate fresh leaf growth by cutting back the flowers.

Recipe of the week

Blackened Beef Rib-Eye Steak with Creole Barbecue Sauce & Fruity Fennel Slaw

(Serves 2)

For the Creole barbecue sauce
- 200 ml (7 fl oz) carton of pineapple juice
- 15ml (1tablespoon) tomato ketchup
- 30ml (2 tablespoons) mango chutney
- 15ml (1 tablespoon) cider vinegar

For the fruity fennel slaw
- 1 mango
- 1 papaya
- ½ fennel bulb
- Juice of ½ a lime
- 15 ml (1tablespoon) chopped mint
- 2 lean thick beef rib eye or sirloin steaks
- 10 ml (2 teaspoons) black peppercorns
- 2.5 ml (½ teaspoon) dried red chilli flakes
- 2.5 ml (½ teaspoon) mustard seeds

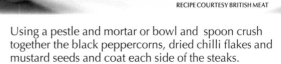

RECIPE COURTESY BRITISH MEAT

To make the Creole barbecue sauce
Place the pineapple juice, tomato ketchup, mango chutney and cider vinegar in a saucepan, bring to the boil and simmer to reduce for about 10 minutes or until thickened and syrupy.

To make the fruity fennel slaw
Peel and slice the mango and papaya and place in a bowl. Finely slice the fennel bulb and plunge into boiling water and then cold water. Drain and add to the fruit mixture along with the lime juice and mint. Mix together and chill.

Using a pestle and mortar or bowl and spoon crush together the black peppercorns, dried chilli flakes and mustard seeds and coat each side of the steaks.

Cook steaks on a preheated grill, griddle or barbecue:
- 2-3 minutes per side for rare
- 4-5 minutes per side for medium
- 6-7 minutes per side for well done

Serve each steak with a dipping bowl of the Creole barbecue sauce and a large spoonful of fruity fennel slaw

Well I never…

'In a bowl to sea went wise men three,
On a brilliant night in June:
They carried a net, and their hearts were set
On fishing up the moon'.
The Wise Men of Gotham –Thomas Love Peacock

Meet my pet

My cat, Mittens, is just like her Mum – she covers up how much she really weighs!
Laurie Walker, Harrogate

Mittens watching her weight

Your June health

Make the most of the warmer days by taking some exercise outdoors. Staying active helps cut your risk of heart disease and diabetes, and according to 2006 research from America, it could also reduce your risk of dementia by 40 per cent. Even gentle activity is good, so try walking, cycling or playing in the park with your grandchildren.

Recipe of the week

Easy Blueberry Brulée
(Serves 4)

- 284 ml (approx ½ pint) soured cream
- 500 g (1¼ lb) virtually fat-free fromage frâis
- 150 g (5 oz) unrefined caster sugar
- 4 drops of vanilla extract
- 225 g (8 oz) blueberries
- 25 g (1 oz) blanched almonds, roughly chopped and toasted
- 3 tablespoons water

1 Mix together the soured cream, fromage frâis, 50 g (2 oz) of the caster sugar and the vanilla extract. Divide the mixture between 4 shallow glass dessert bowls.
2 Meanwhile, place the rest of the sugar in a small saucepan and add the water. Stir together to dissolve the sugar then bring the mixture to the boil. Boil rapidly for about 10 minutes until the mixture turns into a golden-brown caramel.
3 Scatter the blueberries over the fromage frâis mixture in the bowls. Add the almonds to the caramel and then drizzle it over the blueberries. Serve the brulées straight away, cracking the caramel with a spoon.

RECIPE COURTESY THE DAIRY COUNCIL

Healthy herbs

Parsley

One herb that everyone recognises is parsley – it has been used for centuries and is popular as a garnish and flavouring because of its characteristic taste. Parsley is a hardy biennial but, since only the leaves are important, it's usually grown as an annual. In the garden it looks great as edging. Pick the leaves when they're large enough and use fresh or dried – continual harvesting will encourage young growth. If you want fresh leaves during the winter then lift a small clump and grow on in a container on a windowsill. Botanical name – *Petroselinum crispum*
■ **Tip:** Chewing parsley may help cure bad breath.

My Dad

Looking at my father, Jim's, presentation watch from his employer, the inscription reads, 'To J H Hillyer in recognition of his long service with J W Singer & Sons Ltd, 1914-1959'. Forty-five years, that sums up my father completely, as he was a loyal and conscientious worker.

Father also had a great talent as an accomplished pianist. He took on the temporary role as accompanist to Dorothy Ward, a well-known stage artiste of the day. He did so well she wanted him to turn professional but he declined, as he had plans to get married.

Setting up a small orchestra in Frome, he said he enjoyed playing at Longleat House where the present Lord Bath's father reigned supreme. How proud he was that he was the first musician in Frome to play It's A Long Way To Tipperary which had just been published during the First World War.

In the 1920s, he often accompanied the silent films at Frome's Picture Palace. This suited me because I was allowed in for nothing to the Saturday matinees!

Trevor's father, Jim

Trevor Hillyer, Trowbridge, Wilts

Well I never…

And more names:
Woody Allen's real name is Allen Stewart Konigsberg; Lauren Bacall is really Betty Joan Perske; George Michael is Georgios Kyriacos Panayiotou and Stevie Wonder is Steveland Judkins.

That special song

At five years of age I went to singing (mine still leaves a lot to be desired!) and dancing classes. For some reason, come the annual children's show, my Mum couldn't come and so my aunt took her place.

My song was Bye Bye Blackbird, sung with the accompanying actions. When it was over and we got home, my aunt said to my Mum, Ada, 'I was ashamed to admit she was ours – keep your money in your pocket in future!'

This 'damning praise' was re-told by my aunt on many occasions when I was young – even to any boyfriend I brought home. As I got older, it became a source of amusement to me, and even now, at 85 – it still raises a laugh!

Betty Burge, London

Top of the hit parade!

15 Jun 1956:
Pat Boone
I'll Be Home

17 Jun 1965:
Elvis Presley
Crying In The Chapel

11 Jun 1969:
Beatles
The Ballad Of John And Yoko

Top Tip

Put newspaper or plastic film wrap on the top of cupboards and wardrobes, they will collect the dust and then be thrown away to save time
Carol Donnelly, Wakefield

My Dad

My Dad had a great influence on my interests that I have continued with to this day – gardening, photography, music and writing. For a long time, I was unable to have a piano in my various homes but I always took 'our' box of sheet music from house to house in hopes.

Then, when my husband sadly died in 2004, I bought a secondhand piano and renewed my interest. I thank my Dad for paying out all those years ago so I could learn to play.

His early years were not easy, being one of 13 children but he was a hard-working, talented man. His memory grows fonder with the years and I realise his true value in my life.

Drina Brockenbrow, High Wycombe, Bucks

Left: Drina's Dad in the 1940s
Above: Drina and her Dad taken around 1980

Healthy herbs
Lemon balm

You'll adore lemon balm – it's one of the easiest plants to grow and its aromatic leaves smell strongly of lemon when crushed – something you will do every time you walk by! It's used medicinally for many conditions including bronchial inflammation, earache, fever, headaches, high blood pressure, influenza, mood disorders and palpitations and also to treat anxiety, insomnia and stress. Pick the leaves and use immediately in salads, with fruit or, rubbed on the bare skin, as a natural insect repellent. Botanical name – *Melissa officinalis*
■ **Tip:** Studies have shown that lemon balm may help improve the memory and lengthen the attention span of those suffering from Alzheimer's disease.

Well I never…

It is permitted to bowl underarm in first-class cricket if both teams agree before the match.

Meet my pet

Meet Holly, my Cocker Spaniel, who can recognise the postman's steps from the bottom of the road. She waits by the letter box and by the time I return home from work, Holly has diligently taken each piece of post upstairs and laid it (untorn) on the landing.

When my husband was alive we used to have an evening paper, and it was a race to see who could retrieve it first as, instead of giving it to my husband, Holly would charge upstairs and leave it on the landing.

I've not yet trained her to sort the bills out!

Sandra Smith, Halesowen, W Mids

Sandra and Holly

Dear Diary
May 1998

A special entry this month, as it was my Graduation Day from the Open University. At the age of 65, I gained an Honours Degree in Social Sciences.

Helen on Graduation Day

Looking back, I must have been mad or very thirsty for learning. Essay writing and completing assignments for my tutor was time-consuming. And during the summer months, while everyone was enjoying leisurely weekends, I was indoors wrestling with set books and course units.

The graduation ceremony took place in the McEwan Hall in Edinburgh, and I received my certificate from Betty Boothroyd, Chancellor of the OU.

Helen Gibb, Penicuik, Midlothian

Top of the hit parade!

23 Jun 1960:
Eddie Cochran
Three Steps To Heaven

22 Jul 1965:
Byrds
Mr Tambourine Man

23 Jun 1966:
The Beatles
Paperback Writer

Top Tip

Cut old tights into strips and use them as a much kinder way to tie plants than string.
H Thompson, Wallington

Recipe of the week

Warm Asparagus, Griddled Chicken & Feta Salad with Red Pepper & Chilli Dressing

(Serves 2)
- 1 bundle British asparagus
- 2 tablespoons olive oil
- 350 g (12 oz) chicken fillets, cut into strips
- 100 g (4 oz) Feta cheese, crumbled
- 8 cherry tomatoes, halved

For the dressing
- 2 tablespoons olive oil
- 1 tablespoons white wine vinegar
- 1 clove garlic crushed
- 1 whole roasted red pepper, peeled and seeded
- 2 tablespoons sweet chilli sauce
- Sea salt & black pepper

1 Clean the asparagus and trim any white ends or peel with a vegetable peeler, cut each spear in half and steam for three minutes.
2 Heat 2 tablespoons olive oil in a heavy-based frying pan and add chicken fillets. Cook for two minutes each side until golden brown.
3 Meanwhile put the dressing ingredients into a food processor and process until roughly blended.
4 Arrange the asparagus, chicken, Feta and cherry tomatoes in a large serving dish and drizzle with the red pepper and chilli dressing. Serve with warm bread or steamed new potatoes.

RECIPE COURTESY WWW.BRITISH-ASPARAGUS.CO.UK

Recipe of the week

Rocky Road Bars

(Makes 16 bars)
- 225 g (8 oz) unsalted butter
- 100 g (4 oz) plain chocolate, broken into pieces
- 2 tablespoons Lyle's Golden Syrup
- 2 tablespoons cocoa powder
- 2 tablespoons caster sugar
- 100 g (4 oz) Maltesers
- 100 g (4 oz) mixed milk and white chocolate chips
- 100 g (4 oz) mini marshmallows
- 225 g (8 oz) ginger biscuits, broken into pieces
- Icing sugar to dust

1 Line a 20 cm (8 inch) square cake tin with baking parchment.
2 In a small pan heat the butter, plain chocolate, Golden Syrup, sugar and cocoa powder. Once melted together leave to cool for 10 minutes.
3 In a large bowl place the Maltesers, milk and white chocolate chips, mini marshmallows and ginger biscuits and bind together with the melted chocolate sauce.
4 Pour into the lined tin and leave to set in the fridge for a minimum of 2 hours. Remove from cake tin and slice into 16 snack-sized bars. Dust with icing sugar to serve.

RECIPE COURTESY TATE & LYLE

Well I never...

'A man is a success if he gets up in the morning and goes to bed at night, and in between he does what he wants to do'.
Bob Dylan

Healthy herbs

Garlic

Garlic has scientifically-proven medicinal and antibacterial properties. A natural antibiotic, it contains sulphur compounds which detoxify the body, boost the immune system and lower blood pressure.

Garlic capsules are taken to reduce colds, coughs and bronchitis, yet you can grow it easily in the garden. And what's more, its antioxidant properties may help reduce the ageing process by mopping up harmful free radicals – whatever they are! So we should all grow it, eat it and ignore the garlic breath that ensues.

Botanical name – *Allium sativum*
■ **Tip:** Use the leaves in salads – you don't just have to eat the cloves.

Top Tip

When making up your hanging baskets, place a saucer or small plant tray in the bottom to keep the roots moist.
Arthur Barrett, Thatcham

My Dad

My Dad was special. I was the second youngest in a family of six – four girls and two boys. I suffered with many ear infections as a child and nearly lost my life when I was nine, but my dad was always around for me – I was the weakest link, I think.

This continued throughout my life as I struggled through school and he helped me with my homework. When I started to learn to drive he would run alongside my scooter after just having come home from a long day at work.

When we went on holiday, he would say, 'Sixpence to the first one to spot a Rolls-Royce, or score a hole in one on the putting green.' And I'll always remember his weekly treat which was two tins of Golden Virginia, three green papers and two boxes of filter tips – his one and only expense.

Sadly my Dad passed away when he was only 67 and although it's now 30 years ago, it seems like only yesterday and I miss him so much.

Pamela Moore, Ilminster, Somerset

Pamela with her Dad (Ernest), brother Peter, and little Gillian on the beach at Clacton in 1952

That special song

My wife and I first met – three or four times - when we were 15 years of age at the swimming pool.

On our first proper date to the flicks I asked Mabel what she'd be wearing, as I wouldn't be able to recognise her with her clothes on! I will never forget her outfit – a red two-piece with black edges.

We courted for three years and married in 1955, both aged 19. Like many couples, everybody told us we were far too young to get married. And about this time Nat 'King' Cole brought out Too Young.

*'They tried to tell us we're too young,
Too young to really be in love…'*

We celebrated our Golden Wedding anniversary in 2005!

Mabel and Clarry Bullough, Castleford, W Yorks

Above: Clarry and Mabel in 1955
Left: Clarry and Mabel today

Top of the hit parade!

28 Jul 1960:
Cliff Richard
Please Don't Tease

29 Jun 1961:
Del Shannon
Runaway

28 Jun 1962:
Mike Sarne with Wendy Richard
Come Outside

On location at Groombridge Place

Idyllic home for Elizabeth Bennett

After scouring the country for a suitable property, the location manager for Pride and Prejudice (2005) settled for the 'immense charm' of Groombridge Place, Kent, which appears in the film as Longbourn, home of the Bennett family.

Its owner, Justin Bodle, says: "To see Groombridge in June with the roses in full bloom or in the summer at dusk with the light across the lake is to feel this could only ever be England." Along with the Enchanted Forest, the award-winning gardens are the star attraction of this seventeenth century moated manor house, four miles from Tunbridge Wells.

First laid out when the house was built, the garden was designed as a series of 'outside rooms'. In the early part of the last century beautiful wrought iron gates and stone urns were introduced and, more recently, the Knot Garden, the White Rose Garden and the Peacock Walk were created.

The central pathway through the garden leads along the Apostle Walk, so called because it is bordered on each side by 12 drum yews, thought to have survived from the original planting of 1674. The pathway was a major feature in the film The Draughtsman's Contract, released in 1983. The film is commemorated by The Draughtsman's Lawn which features many ornamental trees including a white mulberry planted in 1993 to recall Groombridge's connection with the smuggling trade.

A door leads into The Secret Garden where the waters of the stream trickle over rocks to feed the moat. On a hot summer day, it is a shady and peaceful spot. It was here that Philip Packer, who built Groombridge Place, died while sitting and reading a book in 1686. Centuries later, Groombridge was often visited by Sir Arthur Conan Doyle who renamed it Birlstone Manor in his book The Valley of Fear.

■ *For further information, phone 01892 861444 or visit the website www.groombridge.co.uk*

Remember when…
Doorstep delivery

Estella Granger of Witney, Oxfordshire, recalls yesterday's tradesmen

Growing up in North Kensington in London, the earliest milk delivery I can remember was from a four-wheeled cart carrying a large churn. Round the sides of the cart were hung small cans with flip-up lids that were pint and half-pint measures. These could be kept and returned the next day or you could have the milk transferred to your own jug.

The baker had a cart with a wooden hood to protect its contents. He would fill a large basket with a selection of loaves and bring it to the door for you to make your choice.

Another caller who was eagerly awaited was the Carbolic Man.

Mother used to take out a jam jar and buy two pennyworth of carbolic. This was then diluted and used for swilling the yard, as well as for pouring down the toilet and outside drains to keep them smelling fresh.

Coal was always brought round in a cart pulled by a horse. The coal merchant came every week, calling out his wares as he passed up the street. The coal was tipped directly into your cellar. Anyone who had a bit of a garden would dash out and gather up any manure that the horse deposited.

One caller we children particularly liked was the water cart which, in the hot summer months, would spray the roads to

Estella as a two year old

settle the dust. If we got too near – as we usually did – we would get sprayed, too.

A couple of times a year, a family of gypsies called. They sold wooden pegs as well as brightly coloured mats. Mother always bought one of these to put in front of the hearth in the kitchen and the old one it replaced was moved to the scullery.

A proper wind up!

Margaret Tuckwell dreamed of having a proper record player to hear the latest pop music, and suddenly it seemed her Mum had the answer…

Margaret (left) and Rita (right) in the 1960s

Below, right: Mr and Mrs Worrall, givers of the gramophone

It was 1959 and I was 13 years old. Elvis, Cliff and the Everly Brothers were the latest teenage heart-throbs to get my newly discovered hormones leaping about all over the place as I listened to their voices singing romantic love songs on Radio Luxembourg.

The radio was all right but, oh, how I longed to have my own record player! It was okay being able to fantasise when I heard Elvis singing One Night With You but the fantasy was rather spoilt when the next record they put on was Lonnie Donegan asking me if 'my chewing gum had lost its flavour on the bed post overnight'? I ask you!

My best friend, Rita, had the latest thing in record players, and most Saturday mornings would find us in the record departments of the big stores where we'd ask them to play the records that were just out while we listened to them in soundproof booths.

Then Rita would decide which one she wanted, buy it, then we'd spend the rest of the day in her bedroom, playing records, practising our jive or just weaving dreams about us and Elvis! Then I had to go home and make do with whatever the radio had to offer.

My family wasn't particularly well off and although I'd asked my parents if I could have a record player, it was no real surprise to be told that we couldn't afford it.

However, my Mum worked as a cleaner for an elderly couple – Mr and Mrs Worrall – and one day she came home to tell me the Worralls were moving to Ireland and had asked Mum if I would like to have their record player.

I was so excited and could hardly wait until the following Friday when their son was going to deliver it. My school lessons were wasted that day as I concentrated on what record I'd buy on my next trip to town.

That afternoon I raced home from school, charged into the front room and… oh dear, the bubble that had surrounded me suddenly burst. On the table was a wooden box with a record turntable in it. It also had a winding handle and a small snuff-sized box containing replacement needles! "There you are," Mum's voice broke into my numbed brain. "Mrs Worrall has even sent you a few records as well, isn't that kind of her?"

I walked over to the table, not daring to speak in case my voice betrayed my disappointment. After all it wasn't Mum's fault. I was a late arrival in our household and she was now in her late 50s with more important things to think about than keeping abreast with the latest music technology.

To her a record player simply needed a turntable and a needle, records were round and black and to try and explain the difference between 78s, 45s and 33s was pointless. So I assured her it was great and to prove it I wound it up and put on the records that Mrs Worrall had so 'kindly' sent me.

I had the choice of three records: Little Brown Jug, When Father Painted The Parlour and Let Him Go, Let him Tarry. The only source of real entertainment that they gave me was when the player began to wind down and all the words came out very slowly in a very deep voice, but they posed no threat to my heroes. Suddenly listening to Radio Luxembourg didn't seem quite such a bad thing after all…

Sunday

1

Thursday

12

**Battle of the Boyne
(Bank Holiday N Ireland)**

Monday

2

Friday

13

Tuesday

3

Hampton Court Flower Show begins

Saturday

14

Wednesday

4

**American Independence Day
Henley Royal Regatta begins**

Sunday

15

St. Swithun's Day (aka Swithin's Day)

Thursday

5

Monday

16

Friday

6

Tuesday

17

Saturday

7

Wednesday

18

Sunday

8

Thursday

19

Tatton Park Flower Show begins

Monday

9

Friday

20

Tuesday

10

Saturday

21

Wednesday

11

Sunday

22

Monday **23**	Saturday **28**
Tuesday **24**	Sunday **29**
Wednesday **25**	Monday **30**
Thursday **26**	Tuesday **31**
Friday **27**	

Seaside Memories

Candy floss and lollies,
Burgers, chips and beers,
The sights and sounds of seasides
I've remembered through the years.

Sandwiches with sand in,
Ice creams dripping fast.
The sights and sounds of seasides
I remember from my past.

Donkey rides and deckchairs,
Paddling in the sea,
The sights and sounds of seasides
– Sticky buns for tea.

These memories I'll keep with me
Until I'm old and grey.
The sights and sounds of seasides
I'll remember every day.

Mrs Chris Bishop, Halstead, Essex

PIC: PUZANT APKARIAN/MASTERFILE

My Dad

I was born in 1927, and I had two older brothers. Dad kept our local electric sub-station running and as we hadn't much money, had no holidays.

He would take me down to our local jetty and we would have a trip out in one of the motor boats which took holidaymakers for trips round the bay. Then we would go into Margate, to the Dreamland Amusement Park which I loved.

We'd then go on to the seafront to feed the gulls. I remember one bird swooping so low over Dad's head that it knocked his trilby off over the cliff and down onto the beach. We were laughing all the way down on to the beach to pick it up.

Miss June R Davis, Broadstairs, Kent

Right: Three-year-old June with her Dad, Tom, in 1930

Top Tip

Rather than struggling to drain the saucepan after boiling potatoes, I use a chip pan basket that fits inside.

Tilly Simmons, Cardiff

Your July health

Bothered by feeling hot and sweaty? Sage can help reduce perspiration, so add the herb to your cooking or sip fragrant sage tea. Sprinkle bicarbonate of soda into your shoes to absorb sweat, and use a soap made with anti-bacterial tea tree oil in the bath.

Meet my pet

Sam was a small blue, grey and white six-week-old budgie when he came to us. From the start he was mischievous, trying to escape when we went to put in clean food.

Three weeks later and Sam got his way – we trained him to come onto our finger. At first walking on the floor playing with his ball was far more interesting than flying, but he then realised that he had a whole room in which to fly.

Sam's favourite TV programmes were football and motor racing, and he'd bounce on top of his cage with enjoyment when we put on rock and roll music.

He died at ten-and-a-half years, having had a wonderful budgie life.

Linda Hart, Romford, Essex

Meet Sam the budgie

Healthy herbs
Feverfew

Feverfew has vibrant lime-green leaves and white daisy-like flowers. Pretty in a container, it's worth keeping a few plants nearby because the leaves are great for curing headaches – the herbalist Nicholas Culpeper sang its praises claiming it was 'effectual for all pains of the head'. You can also use an infusion of the leaves as a household disinfectant. Plant feverfew in a sunny position in well-drained soil and deadhead regularly to prevent self-seeding. Botanical name – *Tanacetum parthenium*

■ **Tip:** Place three leaves between slices of bread (as they're bitter) and eat to help prevent a migraine.

Recipe of the week

Stir Fried Prawns with Chilli Noodles

(Serves 2)
- 30 ml (2 tablespoons) extra virgin olive oil
- 1 red chilli, deseeded and finely sliced
- 2 cloves garlic, peeled and finely sliced
- 225 g (8 oz) raw king prawns, shelled
- 1 small leek, finely sliced
- 100 ml (approx 3½ fl oz) dry white wine
- 30 ml (2 tablespoons) soy sauce
- 1 x 300 g (approx 11 oz) pack fresh noodles
- 1 x 300 g (approx 11 oz) pack fresh cut vegetable and beansprout stir-fry

1 Add the olive oil to the cold wok, add the chilli and garlic and stir-fry over a high heat. Once they begin to colour add the prawns and stir-fry for 1-2 minutes or until they begin to change colour. Add the leek and stir-fry for 1 minute.
2 Add the wine and soy sauce, then bring to a boil before adding the noodles and vegetables, cover and cook for 1-2 minutes or until the vegetables are wilted.
3 Remove from the heat and season with pepper. To serve, divide the mixture between two bowls.

RECIPE COURTESY THE FRESH CUT STIR FRY ALLIANCE

Well I never...

Did you know that the heart of a blue whale only beats nine times a minute?

Dear Diary
July 13, 2004

Elsie and George outside Buckingham Palace

This was a really special day, as my husband George was chosen to go to the Queen's Garden Party at Buckingham Palace. This invitation was for his devotion to Parish Council duties – he was Parish Clerk for 14 years.

There was a big tent in which was a running buffet, which was held from 3.30pm until 6pm. There were dainty sandwiches, cakes galore, ice cream and cups of tea. The Beefeaters made a line ready for the Queen's entrance and as I'm not very tall, people made sure we had a good view of Her Majesty. It was a glorious day and the sun shone. What a wonderful memory!

Elsie and George Croft, Malton, North Yorkshire

Recipe of the week

Banoffee split

(Serves 1)
- 1 banana, peeled and sliced in half, lengthways
- 2 scoops vanilla ice cream
- 1 chewy biscuit, broken into pieces (try macaroons)
- 2 tablespoons double cream, whipped
- Lyle's Banoffee Flavour Squeezy Syrup
- 1 tablespoon plain chocolate, grated
- 2 cherries

1 Place the banana in a dish and add 2 spoonfuls of vanilla ice cream in the centre of the banana.
2 Scatter with the biscuit pieces and top with the whipped cream and a generous squeeze of Lyle's Squeezy Syrup Banoffee Flavour.
3 Top each ball of ice cream with a cherry and some chocolate shavings and serve.

RECIPE COURTESY TATE & LYLE

Healthy herbs

Myrtle

The herb of love, myrtle was dedicated to the goddess Venus. A hardy evergreen shrub, it reaches about 90cm in height and thrives in well-drained soils and full sun – it dislikes prolonged winter wet. It has a wonderful scent and is a great culinary herb. Add the leaves and berries to stews and soups and use the flowers as a garnish. Propagate by taking softwood cuttings during the summer. Botanical name – *Myrtus communis*
- **Tip:** Plant myrtle in a container – it does best when slightly pot-bound.

Well I never...

'Begin somewhere. You can not build a reputation on what you intend to do'.

Liz Smith

Top Tip

To welcome a new neighbour, go round with a copy of **Yours** and a recipe from the pages to introduce yourself.

S Smith, Coulsdon

That special song

Jealousy by Billy Fury is my special song – I was really mad about him and was very sad when he died in February 1983.

It was my 16th birthday in December 1962 and Billy came to the Opera House in Blackpool. Robin, my boyfriend at the time, took me to see him, bought me some carnations and a small box of chocolates.

It was the most fantastic night of my life, the show was wonderful and so was Billy – I have all his singles and LPs. Thank you, Billy, for the music and the wonderful songs.

Sue Simpson, Blackpool

Sue, aged 16 in 1962

Top of the hit parade!

12 Jul 1957:
Elvis Presley
All Shook Up

12 July 1962:
Ray Charles
I Can't Stop Loving You

9 Jul 1964:
Animals
The House Of The Rising Sun

My Dad

Being an only child and the fact that my parents waited seven years for me, I know I was special to them both, as indeed they were to me.

I was always a Dad's girl but as my Mum died at the age of 40, when I was 11, my Dad and I became very close.

I have many special memories of him but one stands out when I was eight. At school, we'd been given cardboard cut-outs of a model to make at home, and mine was the Sydney Harbour Bridge.

When I'd put it together, I asked my Dad where it was. I remember distinctly him saying it was in a country many miles away and I asked him if he'd ever been, and his reply was, 'No and I probably never will but you may, one day'.

As he died when I was 16, he never did go – but I did. When I saw the bridge, the memories came flooding back. Under my breath I said, 'I'm here, Dad', and I'm sure I heard him reply, 'What did I tell you, I knew you would'.

Sue Stevenson,
Buckland St Mary

Left: Fifteen-year-old Sue and her Dad, Percy, taken in 1958

Below: Sue, with 'The Old Coat Hanger' (Sydney Harbour Bridge) in the background

My Dad

My Dad – the loveliest, kindest, Christian man you could ever meet. An accomplished artist, lay preacher and pianist, who accompanied me when I sang solo at our church. He wrote many poems, too.

Here's an extract of one he wrote for me on my birthday:

There comes a time when all ladies
To conceal their age try very hard
And so, your years which have passed by
You will not find on this 'ere card

And if some nosey friends of yours
This private information seeks
My lips will never tell your years
I'll say, 'Two thousands and eighty weeks'

On my wedding day (after he'd told me not to rush up the aisle and get there before the organist had finished The Wedding March) I had to hold him back, he was so nervous!

When he washed my hair and gave me different hairstyles, he'd give them names: Plain Jane, hair combed straight back; Mad Alice, ruffled and messy; Miss Prim, straight and parted in the middle.

Marion Carman, Birmingham

Above: Marion with her Dad, Ronald, at Bridlington in 1952
Right: Marion sitting in a 'sand car', constructed with help from her Dad!

Meet my pet

Biggles ready for a walk

My dog Biggles was born in a cardboard box in the bathroom, one of a litter of six – all different sizes and colour combinations. Biggles came from a West Highland Terrier cross/Jack Russell father, and a Border Collie grandmother.

She was born wearing what looked like goggles, helmet and jacket – needless to say, in her five years with us, she no longer looks like her puppy self!

Biggles is definitely my dog, as she follows me all over the place. She loves her tummy being tickled, lying on her back, her eyes shut in bliss!

My husband, Jim, has a stairlift and Biggles loves nothing more than riding down on it. She waits until my husband is five or six stairs from the top one, then launches herself in the air and sits on his lap wagging her plume of a tail.

She loves getting to the post before us and chewing the envelope corners. One day there was a sample of cat food, which was devoured very speedily!

Biggles is a real tonic, and she lifts our spirits – home would not be the same without her.

Diana Mansell, Banbury, Oxon

Healthy herbs

Echinacea

This is one herb you can't help falling over in health food shops, because it has experienced such an explosive rise in popularity in recent years. Research has shown that it increases the body's resistance to infection – something that the native Americans have known for centuries. Enjoy its large daisy-like flowers – they're a delight in late summer, and try buying the supplement next time there's a cold doing the rounds.
Botanical name – *Echincea purpurea*
■ **Tip:** Plant with grasses to create a prairie-like meadow.

Top of the hit parade!

20 Jul 1956:
Frankie Lymon And The Teenagers
Why Do Fools Fall in Love?

20 Jul 1961:
Everly Brothers
Temptation

19 Jul 1967:
The Beatles
All You Need Is Love

Recipe of the week

Gourmet Ranch Burgers

(Serves 4)
■ 450 g (approx 1 lb) Quality Standard beef mince
■ 1 small onion, peeled and grated
■ 1 large clove garlic, peeled and finely crushed
■ 5 ml (1 teaspoon) English mustard, optional
■ 60 ml (4 tablespoons) prepared barbecue sauce
■ 15-30 ml (1-2 tablespoons) fresh chopped flat-leaf parsley
■ Salt and freshly milled black pepper
■ 15 ml (1 tablespoon) sunflower oil

1 In a large bowl mix all the ingredients together. Using slightly damp hands shape the mixture into four 10 cm (4 inch) burgers. Cover and chill for 20 minutes.
2 Brush each burger with a little oil and cook under a preheated, moderate grill or prepared barbecue for 6-8 minutes on both sides until thoroughly cooked or until any meat juices are completely clear.
3 Serve in bread rolls of your choice with sliced tomatoes, onion rings, lettuce and/or a selection of relishes, such as guacamole, onion or sweetcorn relish.

RECIPE COURTESY QUALITY STANDARD BEEF

Well I never...

'Sir, Saturday morning, although recurring at regular and well-foreseen intervals, always seems to take this railway by surprise'.
W S Gilbert, in a letter to the station master at Baker Street

Dear Diary

June 20, 2005

Barbara meets her grandson for the first time

Phone call received 6.37am (on mobile as arranged) from Yvonne to say Darren was just taking her to hospital, as she'd been in labour since 1.30am.

My husband and I set off to make the journey from Southampton to Swansea at about 11.25am. Arrived at the hospital at 3pm, quite expecting that our daughter would have already had the baby.

A long wait in the waiting area outside the delivery suite, until we heard the first cries of Jack as he arrived into the world at 6.04pm, with his

Dad saying, 'It's a Jack!' My daughter and her husband had called the baby Jack right through her pregnancy, even though they didn't know it was a boy.

We saw Jack about 7pm – oh, what a wonderful moment.

Barbara Johnson,
Southampton

Healthy herbs

Tarragon

This popular herb is steeped in history – it was even used by Henry VIII's much-maligned wife Catherine of Aragon. It tastes lightly of aniseed and, when made into a tea, may have medicinal properties including the relief of insomnia. Add it to salads, marinades and sauces. A herbaceous perennial that reaches about 55cm in height, it has twisted green leaves that are aromatic when crushed.
Tarragon thrives in partial shade and well-drained soils and may need protection during winter. Botanical name – *Artemisia dracunculus*
■ **Tip:** Cut back in summer to stimulate new growth.

Recipe of the week

Chocolate Banana Milkshake

(Serves 4)
■ 1200 ml (approx 2 pints) of ice-cold milk
■ 2 ripe bananas
■ Dollop of honey
■ 2 tablespoons of drinking chocolate powder
■ Chocolate flakes (optional)

1 Just put all ingredients in a blender!
2 Divide between 4 serving glasses and decorate with chocolate flakes if desired.

RECIPE COURTESY THE DAIRY COUNCIL

Top Tip

Sprinkle fresh cat litter in the bottom of your dustbin to keep it dry and fresh smelling.
Carole Groney,
Birmingham

That special song

Anita and Mervyn

I met my wife Anita as we both played Nat 'King' Cole songs on a pub juke box. I told her that the only track I didn't have was That Sunday, That Summer.

"Oh, I've got that one," she said, "would you like to borrow it?"
"Could I call round for it?" I asked craftily.

We've been together now for 35 years and I recall with fond memories the opening words of the song,
'If I had to choose but one day to last my whole life through,
It would surely be that Sunday, that summer, the day that I met you'.
Mervyn Saunders, Merthyr Tydfil, Mid Glam

Top of the hit parade!

Well I never...

'The best way to cheer yourself is to cheer somebody else up'.
Mark Twain

Margaret's father, William, in 1940

My Dad

My Dad started work at 12 years old in his uncle's bakery. He went to sea at 14 on the Red Cross boats, Dover to Calais, carrying medical supplies for the troops in France in 1914. Sometimes, though, the cargo was more dangerous, such as ammunition.

He journeyed to many places worldwide until he met my mother, then settled for working the Channel Island ferries to be nearer home.

We lived literally at the water's edge, close to the harbour, and would go fishing in Dad's little boat in Weymouth Bay and catch pout (eel, whiting etc) and mackerel during the season. He would bring me home little 'presents' in a jar, of crabs, sea-anemones and glow worms and other little creatures.

Sometimes he'd be called out at night to help as a crew member of the Weymouth Lifeboat, then we might not see him until the next day.

He would tell wonderful tales of the places he'd seen; crossing the Atlantic to Newfoundland where the freezing cold air froze between balaclava and skin; weathering the storm in the Bay of Biscay, sailing through the Suez Canal, rounding Cape Horn and marvelling at Table Mountain. How to navigate by the stars and make rope mats with intricate designs.

The best Dad a girl could ever have.
Margaret Dowding, Bristol

Places to visit

On location at Arundel Castle

The jewel in Sussex's crown

Built in the 11th century by Roger de Montgomery, Arundel Castle has had a starring role in many TV productions such as Henry VIII, The Prince and the Pauper, as well as the film The Madness of King George.

The castle, which overlooks the River Arun in West Sussex, has been the seat of the Dukes of Norfolk for over 850 years. During the Civil War, it was besieged and damaged by both the Royalists and Cromwell's army. Restoration by the 15th Duke was completed in 1900. Arundel was one of the first stately homes to be fitted with electric light, service lifts and central heating.

In 1846, Queen Victoria stayed at Arundel for three days. The bedroom and library furniture were specially made for her visit and the Duke of Norfolk also commissioned a portrait of her by the artist William Fowler. Many of the other treasures to be seen at Arundel, which include fine furniture as well as paintings by Canaletto and Van Dyck, were bought by the 14th Earl who was known as the Collector Earl.

Of particular interest to anyone who likes church architecture, the Fitzalan Chapel in the grounds of the castle, is a fine example of the Gothic period. Interestingly, a glass wall separates the Chapel, which is Roman Catholic, from the Protestant parish church. Surrounded by its own pretty garden, the Chapel is still the burial place of the Dukes of Norfolk.

Arundel's magnificent grounds have been open to the public since 1800 but have been greatly renovated by the present Duke and Duchess since they took up residence in 1987. Among its splendours are a Victorian kitchen garden and a rare peach house and vinery for growing exotic fruit and vegetables.

■ *For further information, phone 01903 882173 or visit the website www.arundelcastle.org*

Remember when…
Dear old Muffin

Joyce Patterson of Plymouth's favourite toy was a certain little mule

After having a throat X-ray, I was admitted to hospital to have my tonsils and adenoids removed. Mum put me in the cot bed and told me she would be back the next day. As I trusted her, I didn't cry but played with my plastic Muffin the Mule. With a magnet in his head and another in his carrot, it was possible to make him nod and move his head.

The nurses were very kind and one said I was her special patient and she would take me to the operating theatre and bring me back. The theatre was very unpleasant as a smelly rubber mask was put over my face and I could hear the gas going into it.

I woke up in the cot with a very sore throat but my nurse gave me a drink which eased it a bit. The next day I was given cornflakes and toast for breakfast as the surgeon believed this would help to clear children's throats, but I couldn't eat it.

After using a bedpan balanced on the bed, I was washed and dressed ready for Mum to take me home. When she came she found me sitting by my bed, in tears because I couldn't find Muffin's carrot. We said goodbye to my nurse and left the ward. As we were about to leave the hospital, we heard my nurse calling after us. "Guess what I've found?" she said. It was Muffin's carrot – it had been stuck to the

Joyce loved her Muffin the Mule

metal bedpan!

I went home happy, with the best nurse of all, my Mum, who gave me bread in milk and rice pudding until I could eat normally again.

TV Trivia

Test your memory with this fun quiz – if you get stuck the answers are at the bottom of the page.

1 In Coronation Street, who was married to Phyllis, Renee and then Audrey?
a) Ken Barlow
b) Reg Holdsworth
c) Alf Roberts
d) Mike Baldwin

2 What were the names of Paul Eddington and Penelope Keith's characters in The Good Life?
a) Jerry and Margo
b) James and Mary
c) Jeremy and Marion
d) Julian and Marge

3 In Eastenders, what was the name of Pauline Fowler's first husband?
a) Mark
b) Arthur
c) John
d) Richard

4 In the '60s comedy series Bewitched (right) what is the name of Samantha's husband?
a) Danny
b) Daryl
c) Darrin
d) Darius

5 What was the name of the ranching family featured in the TV series Bonanza?
a) Cartwheel
b) Cartwright
c) Carter
d) Cartman

PIC: KOBAL

6 How many episodes of Fawlty Towers were made?
a) 12
b) 16
c) 24
d) 32

7 The village pub in Emmerdale is called…?
a) The Queen Vic
b) The Rovers Return
c) The Bull
d) The Woolpack

8 Which British Soap was originally developed under the name Florizel Street?
a) Eastenders
b) Brookside
c) Coronation Street
d) Emmerdale

9 Which of the following special powers was not possessed by Sharron Macready (Alexandra Bastedo, left) in The Champions?
a) Telepathy
b) Super human strength
c) Invisibility
d) Superior memory,

10 How did Marty Hopkirk die in Randall and Hopkirk Deceased?
a) Hit-and-run accident
b) Shot
c) Stabbed
d) Poisoned

PIC: REX FEATURES

Molly and the

Recently widowed, June hopes a seaside holiday will help restore her old, confident self

June sat on the single bed in the small room she had booked for three weeks holiday and wondered why she had come. The B&B was nice enough but June had to fight the urge to re-pack and scuttle home. She had always known this trip away – her first since Peter died – would be a difficult one.

'It's a challenge,' she told herself, 'and you've never shied away from a challenge.'

But now, faced with the reality, it didn't seem such a good idea.

Her terrier, Molly, gave a muffled woof as she jumped onto June's lap. "Come on, girl. There's a beach out there waiting to be explored," she said, picking up the lead and a small backpack.

The cheerful blue sky was at odds with her mood, but June strode on determinedly. She refused to become one of those nervous women, incapable of doing anything on their own although that was precisely how she felt.

Molly pulled at the lead,

eager for the walk. The seaside village was bustling with holidaymakers. Families laden with beach games, teenagers talking on their mobiles. June passed an elderly couple sitting on a bench, holding hands. She felt a pang at the reminder that she and Peter would never grow old together.

Without him at her side, June's confidence had dwindled so much she barely recognised herself. Where was that outgoing, cheerful, sometimes bossy, woman she had been?

mermaid
by Paula Brackston

What use was she to anyone now?

She reached the shore and was about to release Molly when a gruff voice brought her up short: "You can't bring that dog onto this beach!" the plump, red-faced man told her. He pointed to a sign, 'Strictly No Dogs Allowed'.

Her heart sank. What was she to do? The prospect of long seaside walks with her faithful little hound had been one of the few glimmers of light on a grey horizon. June felt tears pricking her eyes.

"Don't be ridiculous, woman," she told herself, sternly.

As she turned to walk back, the red-faced man called after her, more kindly: "There's another beach where you can take her for a run."

Clearly she had not hidden her distress as well as she'd hoped. He went on: "Go up past the church. The footpath is signposted. It's about a mile."

"Thank you," June mustered a smile.

The walk was delightful. Hardly any people, just miles of sand, and a shimmering sea. June paddled in the shallow waves as Molly bounded ahead. Ordinarily, she would have stripped to her swimsuit and plunged into the sea, but somehow, without Peter, she felt reluctant. She had always been a good swimmer – Peter used to call her his little mermaid.

Gradually, her spirits lifted. She rounded a corner into a pretty cove and made her way to some low rocks where she pulled out her packed lunch and poured water into a plastic bowl for Molly.

How Peter would have loved this place. Instead of feeling miserable that he was not there, she found just thinking of him was strangely comforting. She rose. "Home time, Molly."

June was unnerved to discover just how far the tide had come in. She could no longer round the corner back to the main beach. Trying to work out if she could wade around the rocky point, she felt rising panic.

Suddenly she felt lost and alone – and stupid for not noticing the incoming tide. As she scrambled over a large rock she banged her shin. Tears welled up anew.

"You silly, silly woman," she said aloud.

Sensing her distress, Molly sat next to her. June cuddled the damp dog. Then a shrill cry startled her. Shielding her eyes against the setting sun, she spotted two girls waist deep in the water, struggling to clamber onto the rocks. The terrier barked excitedly.

June scrambled down towards them. "Hold on!" she called. "I'm coming."

She helped the youngsters out of the water. "I thought we were going to drown," wailed the smaller girl, shivering in her skimpy bikini. Taking a jumper and a cagoule out of her backpack, June wrapped them round the girls.

"Where are your parents?" she asked.

"We're staying in a caravan. Our mum'll be going spare."

A thought occurred to June: "Where's your mobile phone?"

"It's in my bag," the older girl's voice was wobbly, "But I dropped it when we were in the sea."

June followed her gaze; the bag could be seen bobbing on the waves.

"Right," she instructed, "Stay put. You'll be quite safe here.'

She slipped into the water but the submerged rocks made progress difficult. She started to swim. Fear gripped her. What if she got into trouble? There was no one to help her. Suddenly, she heard Peter's voice: "Go on, my little mermaid. You can do it."

Reaching the bag, she put it over her shoulder, and swam back. The phone had remained dry so the girls called their parents, who had already contacted the coastguard. They agreed the best plan was to wait for the tide to turn in an hour or so.

June sat with an arm around each girl. She felt an unfamiliar sense of peace, realising she was still of some use. The old, confident, happy June hadn't died with Peter. There were still sunsets to be enjoyed, and life to be lived. And she intended to live every precious minute of it.

June was unnerved to discover just how far the tide had come in

Wednesday

1

Thursday

2

Friday

3

Edinburgh Military Tattoo begins

Saturday

4

Royal National Eisteddfod begins

Sunday

5

Monday

6

Tuesday

7

Wednesday

8

Thursday

9

Friday

10

Saturday

11

Sunday

12

Monday

13

Tuesday

14

Wednesday

15

Thursday

16

Friday

17

Saturday

18

Sunday

19

Monday

20

Tuesday

21

Wednesday

22

Thursday

23

Friday

24

Saturday

25　　　　Edinburgh Military Tattoo ends

Sunday

26

Monday

27　Summer Bank Holiday (except Scotland)

Tuesday

28

Wednesday

29

Thursday

30

Friday

31

Summer Days

PIC: REX FEATURES

The lovely summer days go by
As swiftly as the swallows fly.
Soft breezes blow o'er hills and dales,
Through ripening fields of corn and maize.
Hedgerows are laced with elder blooms,
And sunlight dances through the coombs.

As evening falls, the sun sinks low,
Bathing distant hills in rosy glow.
The day is done, the country's asleep,
And all around the night sounds creep.
Sweet woodbine clings upon the air
And fills the soul with perfume rare.

Now bats fly by and hedgehogs stir,
Stumbling from their leafy lair.
The badger wakes in woodland sett,
But the dormouse sleeps on as yet.
Yes, another summer day gone by,
As swiftly as the swallows fly.

Mrs Pauline O'Keefe, Parbold, Lancs

Your August health

Sunstroke can be very dangerous, especially if you're older – so take care in hot weather. Drink at least two litres of plain water daily to stay hydrated, and top up your fluid intake by choosing foods high in water, such as celery, cucumber and melon. When you're out, cover up with a hat, sunglasses and sleeves – and, of course, wear sun lotion with at least SPF15.

Right: All aboard for brother Ken, and Margaret's mother and father, Trudy and John
Below: Margaret by the sea

My Dad

This photograph of my late father, John, off on holiday with my mother and brother, evokes many happy memories.

For 50 weeks of the year father would work extremely hard to afford our annual break, and during the winter evenings, would derive endless enjoyment from poring over holiday brochures for affordable and attractive resorts, usually Dorset or Devon.

Generally, we'd travel by train and a few days before our holiday, a British Rail van would turn up at the house to collect our luggage to be sent on.

On the day, the train would slowly snake into the station, until with a squeal of brakes and a hiss of steam, it would stop. There was a mad scramble to find an empty compartment where could spread out. Finally we would arrive, and we would be where my father loved to be, by the sea.

Margaret Jesson, Bridgnorth, Shropshire

Meet my pet

Colonel, a blue budgie, was our first pet and he was quite a comic. He enjoyed the freedom of the living room each evening and would perch on my shoulder, gradually moving down my arm to perch on the end of my knitting needle, making knitting impossible. And he'd land on the top of my husband's book and use the page as a slide.

He loved listening to himself chattering down an empty vase but his best game was when we put mixed coins on the table. He'd carry them to the edge and drop them onto the lino. Half-crowns were his favourite and he'd search the collection to find them. They obviously gave the loudest 'ping' which he anticipated with his head cocked on one side.

He caused quite a stir on the evening we picked him up from the breeder. We were on our way to confirmation class at our church and, safely boxed, we took him along. The other candidates were gathered in the front pews, eager to have a look in the box.

Imagine the surprise when he escaped and flew high up into the beams. The sheer vastness compared to the breeding cage that he had so recently left must have overawed him, or maybe it was divine intervention that caused him to flutter down to the pews, where he was soon recaptured.

His birdsong wouldn't have blended in too well with the organ and the choir on a Sunday!

Mrs Mona Sharpe, Douglas, Isle of Man

Colonel in a quieter moment!

Healthy herbs
Thyme

A really great little plant, especially in containers where it may trail attractively over the sides, thyme is also an extremely valuable herb. A low-growing perennial, most varieties only reach about 15cm in height. Thyme thrives on light, well-drained soil but becomes woody after a time and should be renewed every few years – take cuttings, divide large clumps or sow seeds. Use the young leaves and flower clusters as a seasoning.
Botanical name – *Thymus vulgaris*
■ **Tip:** Plant thyme in gaps between paving so can enjoy the scent of the leaves crushed as you pass by.

Top of the hit parade!

31 Jul 1959:
Cliff Richard
Living Doll

1 Aug 1963:
Elvis Presley
Devil In Disguise

5 Aug 1965:
The Beatles
Help!

Recipe of the week
Toasted Trout Pockets
(Makes 2)
■ 50 g (2 oz) smoked trout fillet, roughly flaked
■ 25 g (1 oz) parmesan, grated
■ 1 ball mozzarella, diced
■ 2 tsp tomato chutney
■ 4 cherry tomatoes, quartered
■ Few sprigs of parsley
■ 2 pitta breads

1 Mix together the trout flakes, parmesan cheese, mozzarella cheese, tomato chutney, tomato quarters and parsley sprigs.
2 Brush the pitta breads on both sides with water then grill or toast until just warm, but not brown. They'll be easier to fill.
3 Cut the pitta breads in half and open out into pockets. Fill with the trout and cheese mixture, serve immediately, or grill so the cheese melts a little for a further minute, allow to cool a little before eating.

RECIPE COURTESY THE BRITISH TROUT ASSOCIATION

Well I never...

Did you know that honeybees can fly up to 15 miles an hour!

Top Tip

Disposable paper vacuum cleaner bags can be emptied and re-used before they need replacing.

D Park, Lelant

Recipe of the week

Berry Booster

(Serves 2)

- A selection of your favourite berries such as blackberries, blueberries or strawberries – enough to fill a tall glass.
- A glass of semi-skimmed milk.
- Mint leaves and a few berries threaded onto a cocktail stick, to decorate.

1 Remove any stalks from the berries.
2 Put all the berries into a blender and pour in a glass of milk. Whiz until smooth.
3 Pour into tall glasses, stirring in extra milk if necessary. Rest the mini-fruit stick on the edge of the glass and serve immediately.

For a change try

- Use a slightly different mix of berries – with their distinctive flavours it'll be like a different recipe.
- Blueberries, stoned cherries and a few blackcurrants.
- Redcurrants, seedless red grapes and clear honey to sweeten.
- Banana and strawberries.
- Adding a little clear honey to sweeten.

RECIPE COURTESY THE DAIRY COUNCIL

That special song

My granddaughter, Milly, invited me to the Mothering Sunday service in March last year, held in Bradley Methodist Church – Bradley is a small village between Skipton and Keighley in Yorkshire.

Milly is seven and belongs to the Rainbows and they stood on the stage and sang You Are My Sunshine to their mothers. I remember this song from my teenage years, so it brought back lovely memories and a few tears. The children sang it beautifully!

Pat Worrall, Ilkley, W Yorks

Milly, Pat's lovely granddaughter

Well I never…

*Tips for the **Yours** reader who becomes lost in the desert (with camel)…*

- Don't drink too much camel milk, as this can be a strong purgative
- To make a fire at night, use camel droppings as they make good fuel
- Curl up against your camel at night to avoid hypothermia

Top of the hit parade!

10 Aug 1956:
Doris Day
Whatever Will Be Will Be

8 Aug 1963:
Searchers
Sweets For My Sweet

9 Aug 1967:
Scott McKenzie
San Francisco (Be Sure To Wear
Some Flowers In Your Hair)

Healthy herbs

Catnip

Some cats go mad over catnip and others seem completely unaffected, but whether you have a cat or not, it's still worth growing. A hardy perennial, catnip reaches 90cm in height and produces heart-shaped leaves that are green above and grey below, and purple flowers during the summer. It thrives in a sunny position and well-drained soil. Sow seed or divide existing plants during spring. Harvest and dry the leaves and use in tea or as a seasoning. Or let your cat enjoy it!

Botanical name – *Nepeta cataria*

■ **Tip:** Hung in bunches it may deter rats from scavenging.

Left: Priscilla and her father Charles in 1948 on Torquay promenade

Below: A prize-winning Dutch window display, Barnes 1965

My Dad

The earliest memories I have of my father are around 1938, working in Rayner's grocery store, Sunningdale. He'd learned the grocery trade through an apprenticeship, and wore a long white coat with long white over-apron, which he changed daily.

The Second World War meant a return to Ashford, where Dad was born. He became a fireman, where he was mess-manager, chef and driver. During the Blitz, he drove 'George' the fire engine, and when the London bombing was heavy, Dad was away for days.

In 1946 Dad became a grocer again, working as a manager for Woods of Walton. While I was at college in Devon, Dad moved again, this time to manage Barnes's new grocery store, which was where he'd trained.

I can picture the shop now, with the provision counter on the left. Mouthwatering displays of bacon, cheese and other provisions. Dad entered window competitions and won awards; we were proud of his achievements and I still have some of his awards.

Priscilla Odell, Hampton, Middx

Healthy herbs

Viola

Wild relatives of the pansy, violas are known for the cheerful faces they turn towards the sun. They're really easy to grow – simply sow a few seeds in the autumn and grow the plants on in a cold frame. Once planted in the garden, watch out for new seedlings – violas self-seed freely, but any new plants are more of a delight than a pain, appearing here, there and everywhere. Enjoy the edible colour they add to salads and the garden. Deadhead them regulary to encourage flowering and trim back in autumn. Pick fresh flowers all summer.

Botanical name – *Viola tricolor*

■ **Tip:** Add an infusion of the flowers to your bathwater to ease any aches and pains.

Top Tip

Use the lids from gravy granule tubs to seal your pet food cans to stop them drying out.

Beatrice Appleton, Bridlington

Dear Diary

August 2000

Seventieth birthday five days away but I've got a suspicion something's going on...

A few friends came round unexpectedly, including my son. He put a CD of the pop group, Queen, (Queen) on the floor, next to it a book about Elizabeth Montgomery (Elizabeth), then a second class stamp (2nd) and lastly a green apple (New York).

Sheila and her son, Mark, on her 70th birthday at the Captain's cocktail party

Then he said, 'This is your surprise, Mum, can you work it out?'. It was five days on the QE2 and three days in New York. What a surprise, and there were tears all round! What a birthday present and what a lovely son.

Sheila Cadey, Grimsby

My Dad

I was brought up on a council estate in Cheshire in the 1950s and Dad – like most of the men on the estate – was employed at the local steelworks. When he wasn't at work Dad was in the garden.

At the back was a long stretch of garden: A small threadbare lawn with a swing, a rabbit hutch and a permanent bald bit where an annual bonfire went. Beyond that was Dad's territory – neat, regulated rows of flowerbeds. Strictly no ball games or cats. His speciality was chrysanthemums of all varieties.

On winter evenings, Dad would pore over gardening catalogues. "How about some columbines?" Mum would ask, "Or some Zinnias?" She always longed for pretty herbaceous borders. But Dad entered shows with his chrysanthemums – and was very competitive.

The build-up to the shows was tense. Weather forecasts were studied, and instructions left for watering when Dad was on night shift. A couple of weeks before the show, paper bags were lovingly placed over them. My job on show day (clad in finery just in case Dad won and I was needed to have my

photo taken) was to sit in the back of a neighbour's van supporting the plants en route.

In the hall, blooms were tweaked and aligned, then we retired while the judges made their decision. Fortunately, Dad was a very good gardener and he won a huge amount of cups – it was my job to polish these triumphs every Saturday!

Wendy Brown, Wigton, Cumbria

Wendy with her Dad's chrysanths, which were a good deal taller than she was!

Meet my pet

My cat Paddy used to hide in the tumble dryer. He also enjoys playing the piano, which is okay – but the singing that goes with it is excruciating!

Oonagh M Gleeson, Ipswich

Paddy in a spin!

Top of the hit parade!

13 Aug 1964:
Manfred Mann
Do Wah Diddy Diddy

18 Aug 1966:
The Beatles
Yellow Submarine/
Eleanor Rigby

14 August 1968:
Crazy World Of Arthur Brown
Fire

Well I never…

One of Mozart's piano pieces required the player to use both hands and their nose in order to hit all the right notes!

Recipe of the week

Stuffed Beef Ciabatta Rolls with Pickled Cucumber and Horseradish Aioli

(Serves 2)

Mini ciabatta rolls
- 225 g (8 oz) lean beef rump steak
- 2 cloves garlic, crushed
- 2 cos lettuce leaves
- 4 sundried tomatoes, sliced

Pickled cucumber
- ½ cucumber, very thinly sliced
- 30 ml (2 tablespoons) white wine vinegar
- 5 ml (1 teaspoon) brown sugar
- 2 tablespoons fresh dill, chopped

Horseradish Aioli
- 30 ml (2 tablespoons) mayonnaise
- 15 ml (1 tablespoon) horseradish sauce
- 2 garlic cloves, roasted then crushed

1 Take 2 mini ciabatta rolls and cut a slit into the side of each roll, making a pocket.
2 Make the horseradish aioli. Mix together the mayonnaise, horseradish sauce and garlic. Cover and chill.
3 For the pickled cucumber, take the sliced cucumber and add the white wine vinegar, brown sugar and dill. Cover and chill.
4 Pan-cook the lean beef rump steak with the crushed garlic for about 4 minutes each side. Shred the lettuce leaves and stuff into the rolls. Add the sundried tomatoes and then top with the seared beef sliced into chunky wedges, plus the aioli and pickled cucumber (if you can't fit it all into the roll serve as side orders!)

RECIPE COURTESY BRITISH MEAT

August 20-26

Recipe of the week

Toffee Apple Cider Cake

(Serves 6-8)

- 300 ml (10 fl oz) medium or sweet cider
- 4-5 eating apples (Coxes are good)
- 110g (approx 4 oz) light muscovado sugar
- 150 g (5 oz) butter
- 110 g (approx 4 oz) golden caster sugar
- 2 eggs, beaten
- 225 g (8 oz) plain flour
- 1 teaspoon baking powder
- 1 teaspoon ground cinnamon

1 In a small pan heat the cider until boiling. Then reduce the heat and simmer gently until reduced by half. Remove from the heat and leave until cold.

2 Peel and core the apples and cut into thick slices. Heat 25g butter and the light muscovado sugar in a pan until melted, stirring occasionally. Pour on to the base of a 20 cm (8 inch) buttered, round non-stick cake tin (not loose-based) lined with non-stick baking paper.

3 Arrange the sliced apples on top of the caramel. Cream the rest of the butter and golden caster sugar until light and gradually beat in the eggs. Sift in the flour and baking powder and fold in carefully until well mixed.

4 Gently stir in the cinnamon and cold cider. Spoon over the apples and bake for 25-35 minutes at 190 C, 375 F, Gas Mark 5 until cooked through. Remove from the oven and immediately upturn the cake onto a serving plate. Serve warm.

RECIPE COURTESY BILLINGTON'S

Well I never...

'Government's view of the economy could be summed up in a few short phrases: If it moves, tax it. If it keeps moving, regulate it. And if it stops moving, subsidise it'. *Ronald Reagan*

Healthy herbs

Angelica

A great architectural plant, angelica has thick upright stems and crimson flowerheads of white flowers during summer. It's extremely attractive to butterflies and has many medicinal properties.

Pick the young leaves and add them to salads, soups and stir fries. The older stems can be candied, used in puddings or stewed with fruit.

Botanical name – *Angelica gigas*

■ **Tip:** The plant is monocarpic, which means it dies after setting seed, so collect seed and sow immediately.

My Dad

My father died when I was three years old, at only 36 and my mother was left to care for two small children. But this story is not about my father – it's about my step-father whom I loved very much.

Joe married Mom when I was 12. He had two sons, one a year younger and one a couple of years older, so our family doubled in size overnight.

He had the kindest eyes I'd ever seen. One of the things I remember about him best was his smell – Carbolic soap and Imperial Leather aftershave. And there are so many instances to describe Joe's gentleness and kindness – like the time I helped him clean the chrome bumper of his new car with a scouring pad, or when I stood a hot iron on the arm of the settee and burnt a hole. The frustration he must have felt but he never raised his voice.

At weekends the older boys went out courting and the Saturday night ritual was always the same, ' You smell like a couple of Piccadilly ponces. Make sure your keep your change in your pocket'.

Then it was over all too quickly, leaving behind a legacy of warm memories of a special friend.

Helen Haden, Solihull

Left: Helen and step-dad Joe on her wedding day in 1970

That special song

It can only be The Beach Boys singing, And Then I Kissed Her. This became special to me when I met my future husband, Dennis, at the Majestic Ballroom in Leeds, on July 14, 1964.

We had 32 wonderful years together before he died in 2002. The song will be as special to me for the rest of my life, just as he was.

Barbara Finch, Chapel St Leonards, Lincs

Barbara and her late husband, Dennis

Top of the hit parade!

25 Aug 1960:
The Shadows
Apache

26 Aug 1965:
Sonny & Cher
I Got You Babe

Dear Diary August 29, 1945

Not so much a diary entry, but a letter to my new brother-in-law, Walter, a GI stationed in Germany in the war. I was 10 years old when I wrote this. Walt died in 1977 and a little while afterwards my sister, Margaret, returned the letters to me. I'd no idea he kept them...

Dear Walter,
I hope you are well. We had some awful weather last night. It was thunder and lightning. We thought our little house was going to fall down. It was going 'crack, crack' above our heads.

Thank you for my bracelet, I love it, it shines lovely... I have saved 10s 10d in August for Christmas presents. I went to the Victory tea up at our church on August 22. We had a lovely time.

Our kittens are getting big now... Well, Walt I can't think of any more because my brain won't work today and it is raining as usual!

With love from your sister-in-law, Holly xxx

Lilian Holly John,
Bournemouth, Dorset

Holly as bridesmaid to Margaret and Walt in July 1945

Top Tip

When sewing on buttons, use embroidery thread, which is much stronger than standard cotton.

Olive Hayward, Stanford Le Hope

Top of the hit parade!

30 Aug 1957:
Paul Anka
Diana

28 Aug 1968:
The Beach Boys
Do It Again

My Dad

Irene (in her new outfit) and her father at the dance in 1950

My Dad was a very good ballroom dancer, and among my early memories are those of my parents getting dressed up and ready to go out to various local dances, while I went to sleep at Grandma's house.

When I was 21 I bought my very first evening dress (after the war years of 'make do and mend'). It was pink and black striped taffeta – full length with a full skirt, and it really rustled when I moved. I made a black taffeta dolly bag and covered it with pink sequins and bought black net gloves – to go without gloves while wearing an evening dress was unthinkable!

So I had a lovely new outfit but my boyfriend (who became my husband) was away doing his National Service. However, I really wanted to go to a dance to wear my finery. I saw one advertised and persuaded my Dad to escort me.

We had a wonderful evening – foxtrots, waltzes, quicksteps, and the tango at which my Dad was particularly good. I wonder how many of today's 21-year-old girls would be able to persuade their 53-year-old Dad to take them to a dance?

Irene Spencer, Carlisle

Ben the Westie

Meet my pet

People often wonder why there's a large shopping bag hanging up on the outside of our front door. The reason? Our two-year-old West Highland terrier, Ben.

He shreds anything that comes through the letterbox, especially the daily newspaper, and any mail ends up with teethmarks, as Ben 'kills' all the letters. Our hall is too narrow for a wire letterbox, so the daily battle continues!

Gwen Spain, Plymouth

Well I never...

The dots and colours you can see when you rub your eyes are called phosphenes.

Healthy herbs
Bay

Everyone should have a bay tree in their garden, however small it may be. Bay trees are great structural plants, adding interest all year round and are available in a wide range of shapes – pyramids, spheres and spirals. Bay is a great culinary herb and can be used in savoury dishes as well as desserts such as rice pudding. Plant a bay tree in a well-drained sunny position and protect it in winter if your garden is exposed. Pick the leaves and use fresh all year round. Botanical name – *Laurus nobilis*

■ **Tip:** Scale insects may be a problem but you can scrape them off with a fingernail.

Recipe of the week

Moroccan Lamb Shanks
(Serves 2-4)
■ 2 lean lamb shanks or ½ shoulder of lamb
■ 5ml (1 teaspoon) oil
■ 2.5 ml (½ tsp) ground ginger
■ 5 ml (1 teaspoon) ground cumin
■ 2.5 ml (½ teaspoon) paprika
■ 1 cinnamon stick, broken in half
■ 150 ml (¼ pt) lamb stock
■ 1 orange, cut into quarters
■ Juice of one orange
■ 1 large potato, peeled and cut into chunks
■ 1 small aubergine, cut into chunks

1 Heat a large ovenproof pan with oil, add the lamb shanks or shoulder joint and brown all over.
2 Add to the pan the spices; ground ginger, ground cumin, paprika, 1 cinnamon stick, broken in half and coat the meat.
3 Add the lamb stock, the orange juice, the orange cut into quarters, the potato and aubergine chunks, and stir well.
4 Cover and cook in the oven at 180°C, 350°F, or Gas Mark 4 for approximately 2 hours until the lamb falls from the bone.

Eat with couscous and a carrot slaw of grated carrot, coriander, parsley and chilli.

RECIPE COURTESY BRITISH MEAT

Places to visit

The BBC's series Stately Suppers – with James Martin and Alaister Appleton – was filmed at the Hall

On location at Kentwell Hall

A moated Tudor hall

Kentwell Hall in Suffolk was first used as film location in the 1960s when Witchfinder General was shot there. More recently it has appeared in the BBC TV serial Woman in White and the film Wind in the Willows, made by ex-Python Terry Jones.

The moated Hall has been owned by many different families over the last five centuries. Its present owners, Patrick and Judith Phillips, have added numerous new features – including a maze and a camera obscura – since they acquired it in a neglected state in the 1970s. The maze dates from 1985 and its design is based on a Tudor Rose to commemorate the accession of Henry Tudor. The

camera obscura can be found in a gazebo on the corner of the moat.

Approached by an impressive avenue of lime trees, the Hall is an interesting mix of periods within an essentially Tudor structure. The West wing, with its great kitchen and huge fireplace, and the moat house are the least altered parts of the house. The moat house is where the dairy, bakehouse and brewery were located and in the upper storey (or solar) there is a 'squint' for the housekeeper to keep an eye on the brewers at work below. The East wing has a fine staircase dating from 1675. Visitors to Kentwell see most of the house, including several rooms used by the family.

Kentwell is known for its yew trees which are hundreds of years old and have been clipped into geometric shapes. Also to be found in its grounds are a large ice house, a rare breeds traditional farm and a cedar tree that was ravaged by the hurricane of 1987 but has been turned into a sculpture representing The Tower of Babel.

■ *For further information, phone 01787 310207 or visit the website www.kentwell.co.uk*

Remember when…
Stars in her eyes

Mrs Vicki Plant of Weston Favell in Northampton found Pat Boone was a real gent

In 1960 I rebelled against my dad by taking a job as a cinema usherette to dodge his 9.30pm deadline for being home. Luckily, he never found out that as I was just aged 17, I was not allowed to work right through to the end of the performance at 10.40pm. When I did reach the age of 18, I resumed normal duties which included being in the auditorium during 'X' rated films.

The Broadway cinema was in Queen Caroline Street in Hammersmith and was ideally placed for us to watch royalty, film stars and foreign dignitaries passing by on their way from London Airport. On many occasions we rushed out with our ice-cream trays still around our necks to wave to the Queen and Prince Philip, who would always notice us.

My most memorable moment was when President John Kennedy and his

wife, Jackie, went past and we were lucky enough to have a bird's eye view of them from the roof from where their progress was being filmed for Pathé News.

Many TV celebrities would pop in for a matinee performance. Tommy Cooper was one of the regular patrons; he always insisted on paying for his own ticket and refused a complimentary pass. Once, the singer Pat Boone came in and bought a circle seat, priced four shillings. Being totally star struck, in my excitement I stupidly sent him to the rear stalls. He was very kind about it and remained where he was sitting without making a fuss.

Working at the Broadway not only brightened my teenage years, it also changed my life as I met and married the projectionist and we had three beautiful daughters.

Vicki (left) and a friend

I'm not speaking to you

Lesley Bennion and her best mate Mary were friends for 33 years, although they did have a falling out that lasted all of one day…

Lesley in 1962 – the sultry girl in white

In 1964 I was 18 and working in the purchase accounts office of a local company situated near Stafford town centre. At the desk behind me sat my best friend, Mary, except that at that moment we weren't friends at all. We'd had our first falling-out in the two years of our friendship.

Although I now had a boyfriend, Mary and I still went to the local Saturday night dance together, meeting up with my boyfriend and other friends in there. In those days it was all live music, and we jived, mainly to local bands, although some quite well known stars of the time played there.

We dressed in shapeless shift dresses, our hair back-combed and lacquered, black-liner-rimmed eyes and almost white lipstick. ("What," once inquired my friend's mother, "do you call that shade? Mortuary?")

That Friday morning Mary had announced that she wasn't going to the usual place on Saturday, she was going elsewhere with another friend. I was furious! She was *my* friend! We *always* went *everywhere* together!

Patiently, she tried to reason with me; that I was being selfish, that I had a boyfriend, she wanted to go further afield, hopefully to meet new lads, but I was having none of it and we rowed.

For the remainder of that morning it was probably the quietest the office had ever been. Office life was very strict then. If the boss had only known how many working hours we wasted playing Consequences, or disappearing to the toilets for a chat and for me to have a cigarette!

Each Friday, just before the dinner break, we were given our wages in little brown envelopes. Mary and I usually went shopping to buy clothes or make-up, and we went to the local market to buy our stockings.

However, this Friday I went out alone. I visited a real old-fashioned drapers, the sort of place that had things in drawers with glass fronts, where you could buy everything from elastic to ladies' corsets.

I bought a long-sleeved, up to the neck, down to the ankles, wincyette nightdress; we had no central heating and no snuggly duvets then, just layers of heavy blankets that weighed a ton and a freezing cold bedroom.

That afternoon, again we sat and worked in silence. Some time before, I'd lost my umbrella but that day got it back again. It seemed a good subject with which to break the ice – after all, it was me who had

Mary as a bridesmaid in 1968

been acting selfishly, I realised. Of course she wanted to meet new lads. How could I have been so self-centred. I turned slightly.

"I got my umbrella back." Mary's reply was brief, but not unfriendly. "Good." After a few moments I tried again.

"Bought myself a nightie."
"And me."
"Got mine from Jeffs."
"And me."
"Mine's yellow." "So's mine."
"Wincyette? With little blue flowers?"

We were both grinning now. Mary delved into her bag and I did the same. We'd bought identical nightdresses from the same shop. We laughed until the tears rolled down our cheeks. We never fell out again throughout our 33-year friendship and her premature death, at the age of 48, 11 years ago has left a gap in my life.

September 2007

Saturday

1

Blackpool Illuminations are switched on

Sunday

2

Monday

3

Tuesday

4

Wednesday

5

Thursday

6

Friday

7

IRB Rugby World Cup

Saturday

8

Sunday

9

Monday

10

Tuesday

11

Wednesday

12

Thursday

13

Friday

14

Saturday

15

Battle of Britain Day

Sunday

16

Monday

17

Tuesday

18

Wednesday

19

Thursday

20

Friday

21

Saturday

22

Sunday 23	Thursday 27
Monday 24	Friday 28
Tuesday 25	Saturday 29
Wednesday 26	Sunday 30

Autumn hues

Cool misty morning, sun breaking through
Gossamer webs, sparkling with dew.
High on the heath, colours abound,
Golden the bracken, leaves red and brown.

Bright jewel colours, mist over the mill;
Fruit for the harvest in the church on the hill.
The altar bedecked with flowers, hips and wheat;
Autumn is here, nostalgic and sweet.

We sing our thanks with hymns of praise,
And pray for happy, healthy days.

Mrs Sybil Stimpson, Penkridge, Staffs

PIC: GARY BLACK/MASTERFILE

Your September health

The grandchildren will be back at school this month, so why not join them in sharpening your brain? Giving your mind a workout will help it stay alert into old age, according to research. Anything that forces you to think, demands quick reactions or requires fast hand-eye co-ordination will make the grade, but the key is to keep it varied. Try crosswords, sudoku, or grabbing your chums for a night at the bingo.

My Dad

I was a little girl, an only child, living in a Leicestershire village in the 1920s, and Dad and I were great pals. I especially looked forward to going out with Dad for country walks on Sunday afternoons after lunch.

Dad would turn to me and ask, 'Would you like to go to the 'Reddish Wood' today or shall it be a walk down the fields?' Always such magical words, my special memory of my Dad.

Laura and her father coming back from a Sunday walk – Laura's dad made the playhouse (left) for her when she was three

He was so well versed in country lore and loved the outdoors. How I enjoyed going off with Dad to pick spring and summer flowers in the wood and hazelnuts in the autumn.

Or there was the long walk past our front paddock along the old Roman bridleway to watch the birds in the hedgerows and see the rabbits play down the fields.

Unforgettable memories of precious Sundays.

Laura Fost, Llandeilo, Carmarthanshire

That special song

Marjorie's 'profile' in her local newspaper, in 1958

I always liked Michael Holliday singing The Story Of My Life and one day, when it was in the Hit Parade, I was humming it to myself at work (I was a telephone operator in Basildon.)

The supervisor of the telephone exchange called me over to her desk and I thought I was in trouble, but she said the local paper wanted to interview a telephonist for their Profile column, and ask her about her life.

So whenever I hear that song, I'm reminded of the day I made the local paper!

Marjorie Cantwell, Dublin

APRIL 3, 1958   BASILDON STANDARD

PROFILE

in which we spotlight New Town workers

A TELEPHONE operator at the Basildon Relief Exchange, Honywood Road, who speaks highly of her job, is **MISS MARJORIE VINES**, of 305, Whitmore Way, Fryerns Neighbourhood. She says: " There is something about an operator's work that gets into the blood. It is always interesting, and I would not change it for anything in the world." On leaving school, Miss Vines had no ambition to become a telephone operator. She started work as a junior clerk in a London office and was jogging along quite happily until taking over the office switchboard as a relief for three weeks. At the time, she did not realise that this temporary move would help shape her future career.

* * *

DURING the three weeks she

ing for many years. Her father is a carpenter working

GPO TELEPHONE OPERATOR

Healthy herbs

Chamomile

Chamomile makes an attractive alternative lawn – the variety 'Treneague' is hardy and evergreen and only reaches 6cm in height. It quickly covers the ground, never produces flowers and doesn't require mowing. Great! A tea made from its leaves can help control travel sickness. Botanical name – *Chamaemelum nobile 'Treneague'*

■ **Tip:** If growing chamomile as a lawn, roll it regulary to encourage the creeping stems to root into the ground.

Recipe of the week

Blackberry and Pecan Muffins

- ■ 300 g (approx 11 oz) plain flour
- ■ 1 tablespoon baking powder
- ■ 175 g (6 oz) unrefined golden caster sugar
- ■ ½ teaspoon salt
- ■ 1 teaspoon ground cinnamon
- ■ 2 eggs
- ■ 50 g (2 oz) butter, melted and cooled
- ■ 220 ml (8 fl oz) milk
- ■ 110 g (4 oz) blackberries
- ■ 75 g (3 oz) pecans, roughly chopped

1 Sift the dry ingredients into a mixing bowl. Beat together the eggs butter and milk.
2 Pour into the dry ingredients and mix quickly for about 15 seconds – the mixture will be lumpy. Quickly stir in the blackberries and pecans.
3 Spoon into 12 greased muffin tins or muffin cases (or use individual brioche moulds) and bake for 20-25 minutes at 180°C, 350°F, or Gas Mark 4, until well risen and an inserted cocktail stick comes out clean.
4 Allow to cool slightly before removing from the tin. Cool on a wire rack.

RECIPE COURTESY BILLINGTON'S

Top of the hit parade!

9 Sep 1965:
Rolling Stones
(I Can't Get No) Satisfaction

6 Sep 1967:
Engelbert Humperdink
The Last Waltz

4 Sep 1968:
The Bee Gees
I've Gotta Get A Message To You

Well I never…

By law, Stilton cheese can only be made in the counties of Derbyshire, Leicestershire and Nottinghamshire.

Top Tip

Have a hospital bag packed ready and clearly marked as such, for those unforeseen emergencies.

A White, Corby

Well I never…

Did you know that we own about 171 million cookery books in this country – and that 61 million of those are never opened. Cottage pie again tonight, then?

Recipe of the week

Special Sweet & Sour Sausages with Cranberries (vegetarian)

(Serves 3-4)
- 1 pack vegetarian (or vegan) sausages
- 1 pack chow mein noodles (use rice or thread noodles for vegan)

For the sauce
- 2 tablespoons orange marmalade
- 1 tablespoon soy sauce
- 1 tablespoon wine vinegar
- 1 clove garlic, crushed
- 1 teaspoon grated fresh ginger
- 2-3 tablespoons dry cranberries
- Pinch 5 spice powder

1 Pre-heat oven to 200°C, 400°F, or Gas Mark 6.
2 Lightly grease a medium-size baking tray or shallow oven-proof dish.
3 Thoroughly mix all the ingredients for the sauce. This can be prepared in advance for convenience.
4 Slice the sausages diagonally and place in a single layer on the baking tray and cover well with the sauce.
5 Bake in the oven for 15-20 minutes, stirring halfway through until the sauce has reduced to a thick coating and the sausages are cooked.
6 Cook the noodles according to the instructions. Serve the sausages and noodles together.

RECIPE COURTESY THE VEGETARIAN SOCIETY

Healthy herbs

Cardoon

A majestic plant when fully grown and rather thistle-like, the cardoon will create great impact in your borders. The flower buds and blanched leaves and stalks are all edible and can be used as a winter vegetable. Sow seeds in spring and plant out seedlings at the end of May in sunny well-drained soil. Botanical name – *Cynara cardunculus*
■ **Tip:** The leaves are more edible if blanched, so tie the mature leaves up around each other and wrap the whole plant in sacking for five weeks to protect it from the light, then harvest the paler leaves in the centre.

Top Tip

When painting, place your emulsion tray in a plastic bag and pour the paint on top, when finished, simply throw the bag away.

C Lancaster, Barton Under Needwood

Top of the hit parade!

Josephine and her sisters with their Dad around 1943

My Dad

When war broke out, my father, being Irish, and Ireland being neutral, was given the choice of volunteering or returning to Ireland.

Dad joined the RAF and because Mum was sick and he had three young children, he was given a home posting and was sent to Woodbury Common in Devon to work searchlights on a dummy aerodrome. We looked forward to his leaves because he saved up his chocolate ration to bring home to us kids.

He was a very gentle man and would sit and read his paper while we 'curled' his hair with nutcrackers! No wonder he was nearly bald! But he had endless patience and never got cross with us.

Josephine Masters,
Tenterden, Kent

Meet my pet

This is an extract from a poem I wrote about Archie, our Jack Russell terrier, to amuse the grandchildren – and those a little older, too!

Archie's tale of woe

I was a naughty, frisky dog
Who liked to chew up things
I'd put the fright up other dogs
And try to bite birds' wings.

Cars and bikes, lorries too
Were all the same to me
And as for ponsey pussy cats
I'd make the blighters flee!

I'd dig up holes in gardens
And rag my bed to bits
I'd wee on all the furniture
And drive folks out their wits.

I had a good gnaw at a wicker chair
It was a family treasure
But I didn't care just what it was
It gave me so much pleasure.

I like to go for walkies
That's the thing to do
It's almost as good as
staying at home
When I've got something to chew.

Love, Archie

PS Things are getting desperate
I've run out of things to do
I've dug the garden at least
seven times
And there's nothing new to do

Raymond L Richards,
Rugeley, Staffs

Archie, the Jack Russell, with a gleam in his eye…

Dear Diary

September 5, 2005

The day I drove and fired a steam engine on the Severn Valley Railway – my 80th birthday present from my husband.

The SVR runs 16 miles from Bridgnorth, Shropshire to Bewdley in Worcestershire, and my present was a half-day Footplate Experience Course.

For each session there are four pupils, and on leaving Bewdley Station, two pupils board the footplate and two travel as passengers in the coach pulled by an ex-LMS Engine 260 Class – a beautiful specimen! I travelled as a passenger with my husband, to Bridgnorth Station, and we were given a tour of the work sheds and signal box.

Then at last, it was my turn on the footplate! I drove first, then slowed to a halt to allow the other pupil, who had done his stint of firing, to have a go. Off we went again, with me shovelling coal like mad, until we reached Bewdley Station.

There I was presented with a certificate and a scarf with SVR insignia (the gentlemen received a tie). A wonderful day!

Mary Bullock, Wolverhampton
Mary, very much at
home on the footplate

My Dad

Elizabeth's Dad, Thomas, on top of the hay. You can just see dark-haired Elizabeth to the left of the farmer in the cart

My Dad, Thomas, was a quiet, unassuming man and so dependable. We lived in the country and Dad was a farm worker. One of my happiest and most vivid memories was at harvest time. Mum would pack sandwiches and drink and at about 4 o'clock we would go off to the field.

The workers were glad to stop and have their well-earned rest. It was a very busy place, with all sorts of farm machinery and beautiful horses all working hard toward a good harvest.

The highlight was hoping for a ride in a cart pulled along by Beauty or Prince. We children would climb up via the wheel (it certainly wouldn't be allowed today) and off we went.

Dad spoke to his horses with much affection and I would feel so proud to watch him on the top of a haystack – to me he was the most important person in the world.

Elizabeth Stiles,
Norwich, Norfolk

Well I never…

'It is always the best policy to speak the truth, unless, of course, you are exceptionally good liar'.
Jerome K Jerome

Healthy herbs

Basil

A rather strongly tasting herb, basil is an essential ingredient in every kitchen. However, it's extremely tender so should be grown indoors and protected from the sun – voile curtains are ideal at blocking out any scorching rays. Sow the seed in spring, cover with perlite and grow on at 19°C. When the seedlings are large enough to handle transplant them and grow them on individually. Use the fresh leaves when cooking and in herbal teas.
Botanical name – *Ocimum basilicum*
■ **Tip:** Pick the leaves regularly to encourage bushy growth.

Top of the hit parade!

17 Sep 1954:
Frank Sinatra
Three Coins In The Fountain

21 Sep 1961:
Shirley Bassey
Reach For The Stars /
Climb Ev'ry Mountain

That special song

Our song was Al Martino singing Darling, I Love You. My husband was in the army for 22 years and we were apart a lot, sometimes for months at a time.

But the Forces Radio played the song for me, from my husband, every week he was away. He passed away five years ago, but I still play the song, and it brings me very close to him.

Edna Wegener, Ebbw Vale, S Wales

Edna and her husband on their wedding day in 1954

Recipe of the week

Apple Cake with Spices
(Serves 8-12)
- 200 g (7 oz) Bramley cooking apples
- 125 g (4½ oz) Fruisana Fruit Sugar
- 150 g (5 oz) margarine
- 2 eggs
- 175 g (6 oz) wholemeal flour
- 10 ml (2 teaspoons) baking powder
- 10 ml (2 teaspoons) mixed spice

1 Preheat the oven to 170°C, 325°F, or Gas Mark 3.
2 Grease and lightly flour an 8-inch round cake tin.
3 Peel and slice the apples. Place in a saucepan with 50 ml (2 fl oz) water and boil until the apples have gone soft. Liquidise the fruit and add 10 ml (2 teaspoons) of the Fruisana Fruit Sugar. Chill.
4 Cream the margarine and remaining Fruisana until pale and fluffy.
5 Add the eggs one at a time, beating well after each addition. Sieve the flour, baking powder and mixed spice and add to the mixture.
6 Add the chilled apple sauce and mix thoroughly.
7 Bake for 1 hour, or until golden brown.
8 Allow to cool, then chill for a few minutes before turning out.

RECIPE COURTESY FRUISANA

Top Tip

When using tinned meat, cut both ends off which allows the meat to be pushed through easily and also cut in slices as you go.   *Raymond Selfe, Newport*

Recipe of the week

Coconut Beef Madras

(Serves 6)

Cooking time: 2-2½ hours

- 900 g/2 lb lean braising (chuck and blade) or stewing (shin and leg) steak, cut into 5 cm (2 inch) cubes
- Salt and freshly milled black pepper
- 45 ml (3 tablespoons) sunflower oil
- 2 large onions, peeled and finely chopped
- 6 cloves garlic, peeled and finely chopped
- 1 x 5 cm (2 inch) piece fresh root ginger, peeled and finely chopped
- 2 red chillies, deseeded (if preferred) and finely chopped
- 30 ml (2 tablespoons) tomato purée
- 30-60 ml (2-4 tablespoons) Madras curry paste or similar
- 200 ml (7 fl oz) coconut milk
- 150 ml ¼ pint water
- 2 small cinnamon sticks
- 45 ml (3 tablespoons) freshly chopped coriander, to garnish
- Fresh coconut shavings, to garnish, optional

1 Heat 30 ml (2 tablespoons) of the oil in a large frying pan, season the beef and brown the meat in batches for 3-4 minutes. Transfer to a large heatproof casserole dish.

2 In the same frying pan heat the remaining oil and cook the onion, garlic, ginger and chillies over a low heat for 10-15 minutes until soft and lightly brown.

3 Transfer to a food processor or mini blender and process until smooth. Return to the casserole dish and add the remaining ingredients except the coriander and coconut shavings.

4 Bring to the boil, reduce the heat, cover and simmer for 2-2½ hours, stirring occasionally. Remove the cinnamon sticks before serving

5 Garnish with the freshly chopped coriander and coconut shavings and serve with yellow basmati rice, naan bread or poppadoms, a green salad and a selection of relishes.

RECIPE COURTESY QUALITY STANDARD BEEF

Healthy herbs

Evening Primrose

This herb is close to many a woman's heart, because its oil has long been used in skin creams. However, it has other claims to fame, both medicinally and in cooking. The fresh leaves are a welcome addition to salads, mature leaves can be eaten like spinach and the seeds can be used in baking. It's also a pretty garden plant, thriving in a sunny position and well-drained soil. Sow seed during the spring.

Botanical name – *Oenothera biennis*

■ **Tip:** Remove old flowerheads to prevent self-seeding.

Top Tip

When draining or bleeding radiators, I cut the top off a softer type plastic bottle so it pushes right up to the hole and prevents spillage.

Valerie Sutton, Birmingham

My Dad

My first memories of my Dad, William, were during the 1930s, as I was born in 1930. He always managed to take Mum and I away for one week's holiday to either Blackpool or Margate, where I always had a donkey ride.

As an ex-regular soldier, he served eight years with the 3rd King's Own Hussars when they were a mounted regiment. So any contact with donkeys or horses meant a discussion about where you put your feet and how you sat in the saddle!

Most Sunday mornings meant a bus ride to Petticoat Lane, with Dad wearing his Sunday-only bowler hat, with instructions from Mum to remember to buy some freshly grated horseradish from the man who sold it from a small tray worn round his neck.

Petticoat Lane also meant a glass of Sarsaparilla – hot in winter and cold in summer – from the roadside vendor parked 'down the lane'. We'd usually cut through from The Lane to Club Row, which then was a market for puppies, kittens, chickens and all sorts of caged birds.

After the war he worked for London Transport at Chiswick and retired from there at 65. He always enjoyed socialising and loved to dance to Jimmy Shand's band. He married three times and died at the age of 82.

William E Marlow, Verwood, Dorset

Above: William and his Dad – possibly shopping for Mum?

Left: William and his Dad at the local gardens

Well I never…

The Mona Lisa has no eyebrows in the painting, as it was the fashion in Renaissance Florence to shave them off!

Meet my pet

We all think our pets are special, but to us our dog Toby is unique. He's clever, funny and is so handsome – everybody makes a fuss of him when he goes out.

For us, companionship and love is Toby's main contributions to our lives, especially for my husband who is disabled. When he is very low Toby senses it and never leaves his side and, if he has a blackout, Toby senses it and stays with him until he comes round.

Although I work full time, I know he's never lonely for he has Toby there.

Toby likes going out for a walk, though I use the term loosely because, as you can see, he rides more than walks everywhere!

Jenny Francis, Fareham

Toby out for a 'walk' with his master!

Top of the hit parade!

26 Sep 1958:
Connie Francis
Stupid Cupid

24 Sep 1964:
Herman's Hermits
I'm Into Something Good

Places to visit

On location at Lyme Park

Mr Darcy's Pemberley

PIC: NATIONAL TRUST PICTURE LIBRARY

Lyme Park soared to fame as Mr Darcy's residence, Pemberley, in the BBC serialisation of Pride and Prejudice. It was from this very lake that Colin Firth dashingly emerged dripping wet from head to toe – and thereby trebled the number of visitors to the National Trust property near Stockport. More recently, the Italianate palace in Cheshire has appeared in the TV adaptation of The Forsyte Saga in which it was filmed as though it were a town house rather than a stately home.

Originally a Tudor house, Lyme Park was transformed by the Venetian architect Giacomo Leoni in the 1720s. The showpiece state rooms are lavishly furnished with Mortlake tapestries, a fine collection of English clocks and carvings by Grinling Gibbons. Four Chippendale chairs are said to be covered with material from the cloak worn by Charles I when he was executed in 1649.

Although the Elizabethan long gallery retains much of its original character, there are now few reminders of the Legh family who owned the house from the fourteenth century to 1946. However, three ancient Greek tombstones brought here by the archaeologist Thomas Legh in the nineteenth century do still form part of the collection.

The house is surrounded by 17 acres of gardens that include a sunken parterre, a romantic Edwardian rose garden, a ravine garden and a conservatory designed by James Wyatt. The estate, comprising 1,400 acres in all, offers some panoramic views over the city of Manchester. It also boasts a deer park dating from medieval times, moorland, and an eighteenth century hunting tower. Perched on top of a hill, Lyme Cage is a folly that is said to contain a secret underground passage running from Lyme to nearby Bramall Hall.

■ *For further information, phone 01663 766492 or visit the website www.nationaltrust.org.uk*

Remember when...
Have a go!

When Heather Hoffman of Milton Keynes was ill with TB, Wilfred Pickles was a visitor but it was not a happy meeting...

When I was diagnosed with TB at the age of 15, I was still very much a child and painfully shy. After 15 months in hospital at Braintree, I spent three months convalescing at Clacton-on-Sea where I had major surgery to permanently collapse my lung.

Sadly, I missed out on all the dances and the fashion for flared skirts and swirly petticoats. And I lost my first love to another girl at school who stole his heart while I was away.

It wasn't all bad, though. I made some nice friends and we jollied each other along. While I was there, Wilfred Pickles broadcast his live radio show from the hospital. Before the show started, he visited the wards. He was accompanied by a brusque matron, nurses and a group of aides. Too shy to say anything, I just smiled from my bed, but as he left to walk away – I don't know why – I said to the patient in the bed next to mine: "Shall I get his autograph?"

Before I knew what I was doing, I ran after him, calling: "Wilfred, can I have your autograph, please?" It was the worst moment of my life. All the faces turned towards me and Wilfred Pickles glared with irritation at my interruption and

Heather's brush with fame

exchanged an annoyed look with Matron. I suppose he was concerned about being on time for the programme going on air.

It took only seconds to sign my piece of paper but he left behind a disillusioned, embarrassed girl, sobbing on her bed with a torn-up autograph. I never listened to his programme again.

PIC: REX FEAURES

Musical Memories

Test your knowledge with these fun questions – if you get stuck the answers are at the bottom of the page.

1 Bill Haley's backing band was named after which Ford car?
- a) Comet
- b) Edsel
- c) Nova
- d) Pinto

2 Who was the oldest member of The Beatles?
- a) John
- a) Paul
- b) George
- c) Ringo

3 Who recorded the song I Walk The Line in 1955, which tells the story of the singer, staying faithful to his wife while on the road?
- a) Johnny Cash
- b) Hank Williams
- c) Patsy Cline
- d) Ray Price

4 Which of these was NOT a hit for The Beach Boys?
- a) California Girls
- b) Sloop John B
- c) I Get Around
- d) California Dreaming

5 According to the lyrics of a 1960 hit from Johnny Tillotson:
When he saw his baby what did he see?
- a) Pretty woman
- b) Walking angel
- c) Poetry in motion
- d) Living doll

6 Can you name the theme song from the Hitchcock film The Man Who Knew Too Much sung by Doris Day?
- a) Whatever Will Be, Will Be
- b) Move Over Darling
- c) Secret Love
- d) It's Magic

7 What was the date of the plane crash that resulted in the deaths of Buddy Holly, Ritchie Valens and The Big Bopper?
- a) March 7, 1960
- b) February 3, 1959
- c) April 14, 1958
- d) May 9, 1957

8 What name is Robert Zimmerman known by?
- a) Bob Marley
- b) Robert Palmer
- c) Bob Dylan
- d) Robert Plant

9 Which country has won the Eurovision Song Contest the most times?
- a) Ireland
- b) Sweden
- c) Israel
- d) Germany

10 Which of the following was not a member of The Shadows (pictured)?
- a) Hank Marvin
- b) Bruce Welch
- c) Jet Harris
- d) Roger McGuinn

The Apple Tree

by Dean Frosoni

Vivian clings desperately to memories of the past but an accident of nature forces her to accept that nothing stays the same

Vivian gazed at the garden through the kitchen window. As her hands searched the dishwater for submerged cutlery she observed the old apple tree bending in the wind.

"Looks like a storm blowing up, Tessa," she said to her six-year-old daughter. Tessa ran to Vivian, burying her face in her mother's apron. "I don't like storms, Mummy."

Vivian comforted her. "They scare me too, darling, but if you pretend to be strong they will go away.'

"Will they, really?"

"Yes, really. Now fetch Tigger's dish for Mummy so I can wash it up."

Vivian sighed; if only that was the way things really worked. Outside, the apple tree was swaying violently and inside Vivian was terrified, not of the storm but of the future for her and Tessa. "Why did you have to leave us, Bill?" she whispered, "I try to be brave but sometimes it's so hard."

She struggled to hold back tears. Tessa tugged at her apron. "Don't worry, Mummy, we'll help each other through the storm."

Vivian dried her hands and lifted Tessa in her arms. "See

that big apple tree? Your great grandfather planted it when I was your age. He said it would be my friend. If ever I had any problems I could tell the tree and it would listen."

Vivian recalled the times she had sat in its restful shade pouring out her innermost secrets. It probably knew more about the tragedy of teenage spots and lost loves than any other tree. She smiled at the thought.

Vivian had been raised by her grandparents in this house and knew every nook and cranny. After they died she had chosen to stay, and when she married Bill it made sense to live there.

The house was her anchor. The world might change but she could always be sure of one place that didn't – not if she could help it, anyway.

Bill had given up the struggle to make improvements. "Darling, the kitchen is ancient," he pleaded, "surely it can't be easy to work in?" But no, she didn't want a modern kitchen.

Another time, he had talked of removing 'that gnarled old tree' in the back garden. She had positively flown off the handle at the idea and Bill had resigned himself to keeping

everything the same.

How she missed him. Like the house, he had been her rock. She recalled the way he brushed away her tears on that goodbye day, her face pressed against the rough fabric of his uniform. "Don't fret," he reassured her, "the war won't last forever. Then we'll be a family again."

A year later came the fateful telegram: he had fallen in battle. Now they would never be a family again. Vivian stood at the kitchen window, silently rocking Tessa. If only she could wrap herself in her wonderful memories, if only Bill would walk through the door and hug her. If only…

Preoccupied with her thoughts, Vivian barely noticed the tree's groaning protests as the gale force wind lashed it. Tessa's shriek of horror as the battered branches toppled over startled her. She stared in disbelief. "No, not my tree!" she cried.

Putting Tessa down, she ran outside. The driving rain stung her face as she ran towards the fallen tree and collapsed in tears with her arms around the broken trunk.

Vivian shook with violent sobs. Anger welled within her. Why was this happening to her? She felt like a helpless child

How she missed him. Like the house, he had been her rock

She felt like a helpless child on a terrifying rollercoaster

on a terrifying rollercoaster ride. Running her hands over the roughened bark, she said a prayer for the tree. She recalled her grandfather saying even trees have souls. Her hair was soaked and her eyes red with crying. She felt empty; her once secure world was no more.

The rain stopped and Vivian felt a small, warm hand touch her arm. Tessa stood next to her, looking sad. "What are we going to do, Tessa?" she lamented, "Everything seems to be going wrong for us."

"Tina's mother likes to paint pictures when she's upset," her daughter suggested innocently.

"Paint?" Looking at the house, Vivian noticed how

jaded the once brightly painted walls were, a water stain marked where a broken gutter overflowed. How could she have failed to notice? It looked neglected, although it had once been a beautiful home. Now she saw it with new eyes and felt ashamed. "I just didn't want things to change," she muttered.

Her gaze returned to the fallen tree, a reminder that change is inevitable. She straightened up and drew a deep breath. "Tina's mother has the right idea. Maybe we could paint our home, instead of a picture."

Seeing a smile on her mother's face – the first for a long time – the little girl stretched out her arms for a cuddle.

"And we won't stop there. We'll mend the roof and tidy the garden and do a hundred other things." Vivian felt a surge of energy flowing through her as if someone had opened a window in her soul and fresh, clean air was blowing in.

Suddenly there was so much to do. As Vivian looked up to the sky the sun broke through the clouds, bathing the garden in light.

"Look, Mummy," Tessa pointed to the base of the fallen apple tree. There, anchored onto the remnants of the stump was a small, green sapling. Several leaves clung to the fragile stem.

Vivian touched the delicate shoot. "If you can do it, so can I," she told the tree. "We're both ready to start again."

Monday

1

Tuesday

2

Wednesday

3
Horse of the Year Show begins

Thursday

4

Friday

5

Saturday

6

Sunday

7

Monday

8

Tuesday

9

Wednesday

10

Thursday

11

Friday

12

Saturday

13

Sunday

14

Monday

15

Tuesday

16

Wednesday

17

Thursday

18

Friday

19

Saturday

20

Sunday

21

Monday

22

Tuesday

23

Wednesday

24

Thursday

25

Friday

26

Saturday

27

Sunday

28

British Summer Time (BST) ends (Clocks go back)

Monday

29

Tuesday

30

Wednesday

31

Hallowe'en

A dream of love

A dream; a nothing,
A holiday romance.
Thistledown offer,
Your single glance.

Was I foolish?
Did I go too far,
Chasing my dream
To catch a star?

A dream of nothing:
A smile, a word, a kiss.
I thought you, too,
Shared my secret bliss.

Autumn winds now blow
My summer dreams away.
But shall I ever forget
That one special day?

Miss Teresa Webster,
Falmouth, Cornwall

PIC: JON FEINGERSH/MASTERFILE

Your October health

The clocks go back this month – bad news if you're prone to the winter blues. Start gearing up for winter now – get outdoors for at least half an hour a day to benefit from what light there is, take a B vitamin complex, and make sure your diet is rich in omega 3 fats, found in oily fish and seeds – research suggests these nutrients can boost your mood. For more information visit www.sada.org.uk

Healthy herbs

Houseleeks

Slightly different from the majority of herbs, houseleeks are succulents, producing rosettes of glaucous leaves and pink star-shaped flowers. They're great if you're less than enthusiastic about gardening because they'll thrive on neglect. Houseleeks will even grow in the cracks of an old garden wall and used to be planted on roofs, hence their name. They reproduce quite easily, so if you want more plants, simply remove any offsets from around the base of the plant and grow on in gritty compost. You can use houseleeks medicinally – apply the sap to nettle stings, corns and minor burns.
Botanical name – *Sempervivum*
■ **Tip:** Plant houseleeks right across the surface of a shallow container to create a tapesty of colour – many have red or purple-tipped green leaves.

Top of the hit parade!

5 Oct 1961:
The Shadows
Kon Tiki

4 Oct 1962:
Tournados
Telstar

That special song

For me, it's Glenn Miller's In The Mood, and was the tune my husband Arthur and I danced to on the night we met in 1943, and we still smile at each other whenever we hear it. And this year we celebrate our Diamond Wedding anniversary. Where have the last 60 years gone?

Dorothy Harvey,
Dewsbury, W Yorks

Dorothy and Arthur in 1945

Well I never…

'The best time for planning a book is while you're doing the dishes'.

Agatha Christie

Jean's Dad Peter (on the violin) with his band

My Dad

When I was a little girl, my father had a four-piece band, and they played to the silent films at one of the picture houses in Glasgow, also dances and concerts.

However, when the 'talkies' came, it knocked all those musicians out of work – a terrible time in the early 1930s.

In the summer Dad took the band to play on the paddle steamers which went to Rothesay and the Kyles of Bute but in the end, he had to find other work.

My other memories of him are taking me to the circus at Kelvin Hall and, every few weeks, to the Empire Exhibition in Glasgow in 1938 which was very exciting. And lastly, of him walking me down the aisle on my wedding day.

Jean Ferguson, Cheltenham, Glos

Recipe of the week

Blackcurrant Muffins
(Makes 6)

- 150g (5 oz) self raising flour
- 2.5 mls (½ tsp) mixed spice
- Pinch of salt
- 5 mls (1 tsp) baking powder
- 50 g (2 oz) Fruisana Fruit Sugar
- 75 g (3 oz) unsalted butter, melted
- 2 eggs, beaten
- 30 ml (2 tablespoons) milk
- 75 g (3 oz) blackcurrants, frozen

1 Preheat the oven to 180°C, 350°F, Gas Mark 4. Sift the flour, mixed spice, salt and baking powder. Add the Fruisana Fruit Sugar and mix well so the dry ingredients are thoroughly blended.

2 Melt the butter, either in a microwave or in a saucepan over a low heat. In a separate bowl to the dry ingredients combine the beaten eggs, melted butter and milk.

3 Add the liquid all at once to the dry ingredients and stir gently with a fork until the dry ingredients are lightly moistened. Add the fruit and mix. The muffin mixture should still be quite lumpy so be careful not to over mix.

4 Place 6 paper cases in a deep muffin baking tray and fill each case with the muffin mixture. Bake for 30 minutes or until well risen and golden brown. Remove from the baking tray and cool on a wire rack. Serve warm.

RECIPE COURTESY FRUISANA

Well I never…

To have perfect pitch means you can name a musical note on hearing it, or you can sing any note asked for. Those who have/had perfect pitch include: Barbra Streisand, Andre Previn, Stevie Wonder, Yo-Yo Ma, Frank Sinatra, Leonard Bernstein.

Recipe of the week

Portobello Mushrooms with Beef and Aubergine

(Serves 8 as a starter)

- 225 g (8 oz) beef mince
- 1 small aubergine, finely diced
- 8 large Portobello or flat mushrooms, stalks removed finely chopped and reserved
- Salt and freshly milled black pepper
- 30 ml (2 tablespoons) freshly chopped tarragon or mint
- 30 ml (2 tablespoons) olive oil
- 50 g (2 oz) soft goat's cheese, crumbled

1 Preheat the oven to 190°C, 375°F, Gas Mark 5.
2 Heat a large, shallow, non-stick frying pan until hot and dry fry the mince for 7-10 minutes until brown. Add the aubergines and the reserved chopped mushroom and cook for a further 3-4 minutes, stirring occasionally. Season and add the freshly chopped herbs.
3 Meanwhile, place the mushrooms on a flat baking sheet, season, drizzle with the olive oil and roast for 3-4 minutes.
4 Spoon the beef filling evenly over the mushrooms and finish with the goat's cheese.
5 Return to the oven and cook for 2-3 minutes until the cheese melts or place under a hot grill for 1-2 minutes.
6 Serve with simply dressed salad leaves and baby cherry tomatoes.

RECIPE COURTESY QUALITY STANDARD BEEF

Healthy herbs

Wild Bergamot

The cultivated relatives of wild bergamot make lovely garden plants, adding colour during late summer, and the plant itself is also rather pretty. Still used as a refreshing tea in the USA, its leaves can also be used to flavour meat dishes. The flowers are milder in taste but both can be dried. It enjoys a well-drained soil and partial shade – avoid cold wet soils and the midday sun.
Botanical name – *monarda*
■ **Tip:** Plant with asters and chrysanthemums for late summer colour

Top Tip

When starting a new reel of sticky tape, put a button on the end to help find it next time.
Dorothy Chamberlain, Leeds

Top of the hit parade!

8 Oct 1964:
Roy Orbison
Oh Pretty Woman

11 Oct 1967:
Bee Gees
Massachusetts

My Dad

Pop was an absolute wizard at mending things, from broken toys to bruised feelings. My overriding memory of him goes back to the early days of the Second World War when my ten-year-old brother John (five years my junior) and Mother's pride and joy, had been evacuated.

Mother was like a tiger without her cub and as the days went on, her temper got worse. I was the prime target and one day she reduced me to tears. I sobbed that she didn't love me.

Pop said, 'Of course she does. I was a proud man when John was born but you... ever since you came into my life I've loved you like no other. I would cut off my right arm for you.' Dear Pop. Those words were enough to comfort me and sustain me through many hard time – and over 65 years later, they still warm my heart.

Joan Spriggs, Solihull

Pop, in 1963, the year before he died

Meet my pet

I had to write and tell you about 'my boys', very handsome brothers Buster and Pickle, who were abandoned when five months old and very ill with cat flu and were being cared for at our local animal rescue centre.

I had just lost my old cat, who was 19 and-a-half years old, so I went looking for a mature female cat as a replacement (being a mature female myself!). I returned with two male six-month-old kittens – the best laid plans..!

They couldn't be parted because Pickles was very nervous and needed the support of his more 'laid back' brother, Buster. Needless to say, Pickles is now the boss indoors, although Buster reigns supreme outdoors - he is a hunter and brings back mice for Pickles.

Daphne Hammond, Exmouth

Above: Pickles with his arm round Buster

Right: Pickles looking down on Buster – 'This is our favourite game, having fun with the rug!'

Betty and David's carriage awaits…

Dear Diary

October 2000

The day has dawned on our 50th Wedding Anniversary. At one time David and I had thought we would never make it to the restaurant of our choice.

Three weeks ago, a huge fire there gutted the kitchens and the beautiful view we should have had from the conservatory – overlooking undulating countryside – has been replaced with mobile kitchens. Nothing's perfect!

It was pouring with rain when we left for our lunch and, much to our surprise, four friends had arranged for us to be taken to the restaurant in a 1950 vintage white Rolls-Royce, decorated with gold ribbons. My, we did feel special!

We had a wonderful time, celebrating with friends and relatives who, I'm sure, were too busy feeding their faces to notice there was no view.

Betty Hancock, Hitchin, Herts

That special song

The song that means so much to me is I Love You Because by Jim Reeves. I'm nearly 70 and I married Billy in 1960, when I was 24. I was only married for 14 months, and he was in hospital for five of those, as he died of cancer at the age of 31.

I've loved the song all these years, and although it makes me sad to hear it, the words sum up all that my husband was.

Ivy Thompson, London

Eighteen-year-old Ivy in 1954

Well I never…

'I think there is a world market for maybe five computers'.

Thomas Watson, chairman of IBM, in 1949.

Healthy herbs

Elder

The smell this tree exudes is enough to deter anyone from growing it and few would recommend it as a garden plant. However, it was regarded as almost magical in the Middle Ages and is commonly found in hedgerows. Elderflowers can be used medicinally and in cooking. Pick the flowers in spring and use them fresh in tasty cordials and to treat coughs, colds and allergies. The berries make a delicious wine but if you're more interested in the garden, then an elder spray is effective against aphids, caterpillars and root flies. Botanical name – *Sambucus nigra*

■ **Tip:** Although elder is only really suitable for large wildlife-friendly gardens, the cultivated varieties Sambucus racemosa 'Aurea' and 'Black Beauty' are lovely garden plants.

Pop – Harry Joseph – at his granddaughter's wedding

My Dad

Father was the original Steptoe – he never ever threw anything away; his old shed was overflowing with boxes, tins and jam jars all packed with nails, bolts and bits of wire. It was an Aladdin's cave and there wasn't a thing that he couldn't put his hands on.

Neighbourhood children were always popping in with broken toys, bent bike frames, old wheels and asking, 'Pop, can you fix this? Can you make a trolley or a rabbit hutch, or a bird cage?'

And Pop would say, 'We'll see'. He'd roll another cigarette, leaving trails of tobacco hanging down; he'd light up, go up in flames, leaving yet another hole in his jumper… Then he'd roll up his sleeves and set to work and always managed to do whatever the children wanted.

Doreen James, Bridgend

Top of the hit parade!

20 Oct 1960:
Roy Orbison
Only The Lonely

19 Oct 1961:
Helen Shapiro
Walkin' Back To Happiness

Recipe of the week

Chocolate Espresso and Roasted Pecan Torte (Vegan)

- 200 g (7 oz) creamed coconut
- 1.3 litres (2½ pints) boiling water
- 30 ml (2 tablespoons) of the boiling water
- 800 g (1 lb 12oz) self raising flour
- 100 g (4 oz) cocoa powder
- 10 ml (2 teaspoons) baking powder
- 100 g (4 oz) roasted pecans
- 300 g (approx 11 oz) light muscovado sugar
- 420 ml (14 fl oz) vegetable oil
- 30 ml (2 tablespoons) espresso

Fudge Icing
- 100 g (4 oz) vegan margarine
- 10 ml (2 teaspoons) espresso
- 100 g (4 oz) cocoa powder
- 90 ml (6 tablespoons) water
- 550 g (18 oz approx) icing sugar
- Few drops vanilla essence

1 Preheat the oven to 180°C, 350°F, Gas Mark 4
2 Grease and line a 27.5 cm (11 inch) cake tin.
3 Place the creamed coconut in a large bowl and cover with the water, stir until dissolved.
4 Mix together the flour, cocoa powder, baking powder, pecan nuts and sugar.
5 Add the espresso mixture and the oil and stir thoroughly, then add the cooled, dissolved coconut and mix well.
6 Pour the mixture into the cake tin and place in the oven for approximately 1 hour, or until the cake feels springy to the touch.
7 Leave to cool slightly before turning out onto a cooling rack.
8 When the cake is cool, drizzle with the brandy.
9 To make the fudge icing, place all the ingredients into a food processor and blend until smooth.
10 Spread the icing evenly over the cake and use a fork to decorate.

RECIPE COURTESY THE VEGETARIAN SOCIETY

Well I never…

A train is cancelled in Britain every five minutes.

Recipe of the week

Spicy Moroccan Pumpkin Soup

- 2 tablespoons sunflower or olive oil
- 1 large onion, chopped
- 2 cloves garlic, chopped
- ½ teaspoon ground cumin
- ½ teaspoon ground cinnamon
- ½ teaspoon ground ginger
- ¼ teaspoon ground cloves
- Generous grinding of black pepper
- 2 tablespoons dark muscovado sugar
- 1 small pumpkin (about 1 kg/2 lb) peeled and diced
- 750 ml (1¼ pints) vegetable stock
- 1 tin chickpeas, drained
- Dash of Tabasco sauce
- Squeeze of lemon juice
- Salt and pepper
- Cayenne pepper to finish (optional)

1 Heat the oil in a large pan and add the onion and garlic.
2 Cook gently for 2-3 minutes until beginning to soften, then add the spices, sugar and pumpkin. Cook for 5 minutes, stirring until fragrant.
3 Pour in the stock and bring to the boil. Simmer gently until the pumpkin is tender.
4 Add the chickpeas, Tabasco and lemon juice. Taste and adjust the seasoning if needed.
5 Purée the mixture in a food processor or with a handheld blender until smooth.
6 Serve piping hot, with a sprinkling of cayenne if liked.

RECIPE COURTESY BILLINGTON'S

Healthy herbs

Nasturtium

Although many gardeners dislike growing nasturtiums because they're a magnet for blackfly, they're still a worthy member of a summer garden. The fresh petals really brighen up salads and have a great peppery taste, as do the seeds and leaves. Sow the seed in spring and plant out the seedlings at the end of May in sun or partial shade – avoid fertile soils or you'll get all leaves and no flowers. Botanical name – *tropaeloum*
- **Tip:** If blackfly, aphids and the caterpillar of the cabbage white butterfly are a problem in your garden, then use nasturtiums as a sacrificial crop.

Top Tip

Simply put a slice of lemon in a dish of water and boil in the microwave until there is plenty of steam then wipe over the inside to clean it.

M Sillett, Marlborough

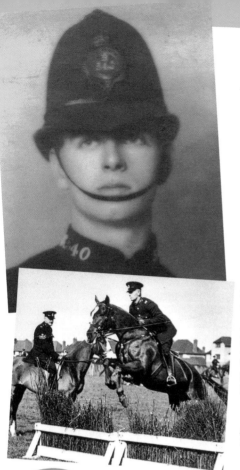

My Dad

My father, Ronald John Williams, ended his police service as a mounted policeman with the Metropolitan Police Service. His lovely horse, Kate, was black with a white blaze on her nose.

My first memory of my father was when I was staying with friends at Thames Ditton, and each morning he would arrive clip-clopping along the street on Kate while I waited anxiously at the window.

Several years later, in 1947, we were very excited when Kate was chosen to be the horse for our Queen, then Princess Elizabeth – to ride at her first Trooping the Colour after the war.

I remember visiting Kate at the Royal Mews at Hampton Court where she was stabled, and also remember meeting my father (with sugar lumps for Kate) when he finished duty at Kempton Park Races.

When he was invalided out of the police force he became Livestock Advisory Officer for Middlesex County Council. He loved working with animals and his job gave him the opportunity to foster the love of animals in children. My father judged poultry shows and rabbit shows and was well known in his field, appearing on TV.

Janet Cox, Aylesbury

Above: Ronald John Williams at the beginning of his police career
Left: Ronald in training, riding Kate

Meet my pet

Here's Lucy the cat, Tarka and Barnaby, snug in a buggy!

I have quite a few pets – guinea pigs, cats, Tarka the Yorkshire Terrier and Barnaby, the Shih-Tzu – and so many photographs of them, I didn't know which to send!

Janet Porte, St Leonards on Sea

Top of the hit parade!

22 Oct 1964:
Sandie Shaw
(There's) Always Something There To Remind Me

25 Oct 1969:
Archies
Sugar Sugar

27 Oct 1973:
David Cassidy
Daydreamer

On location at Syon House

Flora, fauna and terrapins

Just across the River Thames from Kew Gardens is Syon House and Park which is owned by the Duke of Northumberland. Among the many films that have made use of its splendid Robert Adam interior and 200 acres of parkland, designed by 'Capability' Brown, are Gosford Park, The Madness of King George and The Golden Bowl (starring Kate Beckinsale). Numerous TV appearances include Byron and The Lost Prince.

Since the eighteenth century, the gardens at Syon have been renowned for their extensive collection of rare trees and plants and they are now registered a Grade I landscape in the English Heritage Register of Parks and Gardens. Flora's Lawn is dominated by a 55 foot column that dates from 1758 when the first Duke converted a large orchard into a fashionable 'pleasure ground'.

Today, the organically grown herbaceous borders contain ornamental thistles, euphorbias, phlox, scabious and gypsophila. The other principal feature of the pleasure ground is a lake that is a haven for wildlife, including terrapins.

The ice house at Syon was in use as long ago as 1760 when it took two days to fill it with ice from the lake. The ice was used to make ice-cream and sorbets, as well as to cool wine and Champagne for the ducal table.

The crowning glory of Syon Park's gardens is without doubt the Great Conservatory. The 3rd Duke of Northumberland commissioned Charles Fowler to build a new conservatory in 1826, the first of its kind to be built out of gunmetal, Bath stone and glass. It was originally designed to act as a show house for the Duke's collection of exotic plants and inspired Joseph Paxton in his designs for the spectacular Crystal Palace.

■ *For further information, phone 020 8560 0882 or visit the website www.syonpark.co.uk*

Remember when...
Doing porridge

A playground fall resulted in TB of the spine and several years in hospital for Kathleen Tattersall of Accrington

It took three months to diagnose my illness and another three months before I was admitted to Wrightington Hospital. We were given lessons every day so that we would not fall behind with our studies but quite often I used to just pull the sheet over my head and try to go to sleep! I enjoyed the craft lessons which included basket weaving and embroidery. As I missed so much of my early education, I didn't take the Eleven Plus after I returned to school.

The hospital food was good, on the whole, but some of the cooks were better than others (need I say more). Most days started with porridge, and rabbit was a frequent part of our diet – it always seemed to contain small bones. The very large, thin beefburgers stick in my mind, too.

I had two operations, including a bone graft taken from my leg to replace the diseased bone on my vertebrae. My surgeon was Sir John Charnley who later went on to pioneer hip replacement surgery. After two whole years of lying flat on my back, I was allowed to get out of bed and had to learn how to walk again. I just didn't know what to do with my feet. It took quite some time before my muscles were strong enough for me to walk unaided.

Kathleen learning to walk again

Since this life-saving operation, I have enjoyed a normal life and celebrated over 40 years of happy marriage to my husband David; we have three daughters and four wonderful grandchildren.

PIC: MASTERFILE

Word Power Puzzle

Test your vocabulary with this fun puzzle – just match the words and their meanings

	Definitions			Words	Answer
1	Yellow coloured (especially flowers)		A	Anathema	
2	Wrinkled, covered with lines		B	Bibelot	
3	Twilight, dusk		C	Chronology	
4	To be everywhere at the same time		D	Dugong	
5	The study of time		E	Equivocal	
6	The science of grape growing		F	Filibuster	
7	Study of bumps on the head		G	Gloaming	
8	Stone mill turned by hand		H	Haft	
9	Solemn ecclesiastical curse		I	Ischaemia	
10	Plausibly deceptive fallacy		J	Jocose	
11	Person who obstructs legislation		K	Khaki	
12	Nimble, flexible		L	Lissom	
13	Knick-knack		M	Menhir	
14	Humped domesticated ox		N	Nepotism	
15	Herbivorous marine mammal with flipper-like forelimbs		O	Orotund	
16	Handle of an axe or knife		P	Phrenology	
17	Full, round, booming voice		Q	Quern	
18	Full of jokes		R	Rugose	
19	Favouring of relatives or friends		S	Sophism	
20	Dust coloured		T	Turpitude	
21	Deficiency of blood in a part of the body		U	Ubiquity	
22	Curved Turkish dagger		V	Viticulture	
23	Capable of meaning two or more things		W	Whelp	
24	Baseness, depravity		X	Xanthic	
25	Ancient standing stone		Y	Yataghan	
26	A young dog or lion		Z	Zebu	

ANSWERS: 1 X, 2 R, 3 G, 4 U, 5 C, 6 V, 7 P, 8 Q, 9 A, 10 S, 11 F, 12 L, 13 B, 14 Z, 15 D, 16 H, 17 O, 18 J, 19 N, 20 K, 21 I, 22 Y, 23 E, 24 T, 25 M, 26 W

A turkey called Tina

Turkey for Malcolm Welshman's Christmas lunch looked a certainty – that is, until the talented Tina averted a criminal catastrophe…

There is a loud gobble from the wicker basket as I heave it onto the kitchen table.

"What is it this time?" my wife, Maxeen, groans, knowing my weakness for bringing home waifs and strays – but that is one of the hazards of being married to a vet. The house already has its full quota of abandoned cats, a featherless cockatoo and a deaf dog called Nelson.

"Remember that difficult farrowing at Chris Fenning's piggery over at Attleborough?" I ask, unstrapping the lid. "Well, this is Chris's thank-you present to us."

The lid creaks open and a long, red-wattled neck uncurls from within. A large, pointed black beak swings in my direction and a charcoal eye stares coldly at me.

"With five months to Christmas, we can fatten her up nicely," I say.

There is an indignant gobble from the turkey as I scoop her out of the basket in a flurry of black feathers and flailing long claws.

"She's a Norfolk Black. Chris says they make good table birds," I go on.

"Have you thought where we'd keep her?" asks Maxeen as we watch our prospective Christmas dinner peck unwittingly at her reflection in the oven door.

I shrug. "What about the old chicken coop?"

"It's full of fertile guinea-pigs."

"The lovebirds aviary?"

"Elderly budgerigars."

"Ah, I know – the garden shed!" I declare undaunted. "I'll move the ferrets into the garage

until Christmas."

The shed provides a good shelter. Tina, as we call her, is locked up at night to protect her from our local prowler – a fox with a taste for all things feathered.

Feeding is easy. I've never liked mowing the lawn, and grass for Tina is the ideal excuse not to. But as she grows, so does her appetite for pastures new. Her first excursion is to Miss Hastings, the retired post-mistress who lives next door.

"I'm sorry to trouble you, dear," she says to Maxeen over the phone. "But there's this rather large turkey picking my pansies. Is he yours?"

My wife hurries round straightaway and catches Tina trying to decapitate a red plastic gnome. Seeing Maxeen advance up the path, Tina gives a cackle of greeting before trundling into

the petunias. Maxeen heads her off but not before a neat row of dwarf marigolds has been crushed under her claw, and a beakful of geraniums snatched.

The Rectory is Tina's next port of call, waddling through the vicar's rose bushes, clearly enjoying herself but making the incumbent very hot under his dog-collar.

She's surprisingly nimble, despite her enormous girth, and I find her difficult to catch.

The vicar comes to the rescue with a Savoy cabbage. "Maybe a little temptation?" he says with a benign smile and strips off the outer leaves of the cabbage, putting them in neat piles as if arranging prayer books. It does the trick though. Tina is tempted and I pounce on her. She hisses. I swear, and the vicar crosses himself and utters a series of fervent 'bless you's'.

of gobbles from the bottom of the garden as I fumble at the front door trying to align key with latch. When we finally manage to let ourselves in, we promptly trip over Nelson, snoring in blissful deafness on the hall rug.

I don't sleep too well as I dream of being chased round and round the kitchen table by an irate turkey with a knife and fork in each wing.

Tina's frantic gobbling wakes me up, her cackles rising to a crescendo. Is Foxie after our Christmas dinner? I spring out of bed, snap on the light and, throwing a dressing gown over my shoulders, pound down the stairs.

An open back door greets me, a pane of glass broken. I hear the sound of footsteps running away. Too late, Nelson cottons on to the fact we'd had burglars and barks.

Of course, we have Tina to thank for the warning – she saved our skins, so the least we can do is save hers. And certainly we enjoy the chicken more on Christmas Day.

As for Tina, she tucks into a large helping of 'turkey mash', followed by a portion of Christmas pudding liberally laced with brandy. Perhaps, that accounts for the extra swagger in her early morning parade on Boxing Day. Or does she sense her lucky reprieve?

Anyway, her future is now secure. I've been given two goslings to fatten up during the summer. They are quite endearing creatures and provide good company for Tina. As they grow, so does our fondness for them.

So it looks as if, next Christmas, we'll be tucking into boiled ham with all the trimmings.

I manage to curtail her wanderings with plastic mesh, chicken wire and dismantled budgerigar cages. But it means sacrificing the vegetable plot.

"At least it's helping to fatten her up," I say as I watch the last row of my sprouts being devoured.

Maxeen grimaces. "Actually, I'm getting rather fond of Tina," she says. "She gives me a friendly gobble in the morning when I let her out. And she always rummages in my pockets for breakfast scraps. What about having a goose for Christmas instead?"

But I am adamant. Maxeen realises that when she finds the cordon bleu cookery book I'd been engrossed in open at Roast Turkey with Traditional Forcemeat and Watercress; and when Chris Penning's wife phones with a recipe for chestnut and apple stuffing that I requested, my wife realises that Tina's days are numbered.

The Friday before Christmas is the vets' party. The traditional wine and cheese round the operating table. We return late that evening. There are a couple

Thursday **1** All Saints' Day	Monday **12**
Friday **2**	Tuesday **13**
Saturday **3**	Wednesday **14**
Sunday **4** London to Brighton Veteran Car Run	Thursday **15**
Monday **5** Guy Fawkes' Night	Friday **16**
Tuesday **6**	Saturday **17**
Wednesday **7**	Sunday **18**
Thursday **8**	Monday **19**
Friday **9**	Tuesday **20**
Saturday **10** Lord Mayor's Show, London	Wednesday **21**
Sunday **11** Remembrance Sunday	Thursday **22**

Friday **23**	Tuesday **27**
Saturday **24**	Wednesday **28**
Sunday **25**	Thursday **29**
Monday **26**	Friday **30** **St. Andrew's Day**

We will remember

They made the final sacrifice
On land, in air, at sea.
No half measure would suffice
On the altar of the free.

From highlands, lowlands, moors, dales
They hurried without pause,
From shires, hamlets, towns and vales,
To serve in freedom's cause.

Field, desert, jungle, where all decayed,
War's dread death-rattle hushed.
In unmarked graves so many laid,
Before the enemy was crushed.

These tiny isles, unconquered long,
Valiant when all seems lost,
What debt we owe the gallant throng
Who did not count the cost.

Mrs Margaret Austin, Hampton, Middx

PIC: FRANK KRAHMER/MASTERFILE

That special song

I met my future husband in August 1954, dancing at the Spa in Scarborough. I went there with three friends, a girl and two lads.

Barry didn't ask me to dance at first because he thought we were two couples. Lucky for me he realised we weren't, and our first dance together of many, was to the tune I've Got You Under My Skin.

We were together for the rest of the evening, the first evening of our life together.

Sylvia F Howe, Stockport

Maureen and Barry at Oliver's Mount, Scarborough, in 1955

Healthy herbs
Welsh onion

PIC: REX FEATURES

A hardy perennial, this allium species produces large creamy flowers in summer. Pick the young leaves from late spring onwards and harvest the bulbs in autumn. Divide established clumps during the autumn. Cut the leaves into rings and use in salads. Use the bulbs as you would onions in cooking. Botanical name – *Allium fistulosum*

■ **Tip:** Pull up the whole plant when young and use as a spring onion.

Top Tip

Sink a 1 litre ice cream tub into the ground and fill with cheap beer to make the ideal slug trap.

M Sharpe, Isle Of Man

Top of the hit parade!

30 Oct 1959:
Cliff Richard
Travelling Light

3 Nov 1960:
Elvis Presley
It's Now Or Never

4 Nov 1965:
Rolling Stones
Get Off Of My Cloud

Well I never…

'You sometimes see a woman who would have made a Joan of Arc in another century and climate, threshing herself to pieces over all the mean worry of housekeeping'.

Rudyard Kipling

Your November health

Bolster your immunity before the winter colds start doing the rounds. Taking the herb echinacea can be helpful (check with your GP if you're on other medication) and make sure your diet is rich in vitamin C – excellent sources include sweet potatoes, red peppers and kiwi fruits. And wash your hands regularly, as it's one of the best ways to prevent cold germs being transferred.

Recipe of the week
Pineapple and Coconut Pancakes with Golden Syrup and Crème Fraîche

- 250 g (10 oz) pancake mix
- 110 g (4 oz) sweetened desiccated coconut
- 1 egg, whisked
- 350 ml (approx ½ pint) milk
- 200 g (7 oz) can of crushed pineapple
- Vegetable oil, for frying
- 2 tablespoons Lyle's Golden Syrup
- Crème fraîche or plain yoghurt for serving

1 In a large bowl combine the pancake mix, coconut, egg, milk and crushed pineapple together to make the batter.
2 Heat the oil in a large frying pan, over a medium heat. Pour a rounded tablespoon of batter onto the hot pan and flatten slightly.
3 Fry the batter for 1-2 minutes and when it starts to bubble, turn over to reveal a crisp and golden side. Cook for a further 1-2 mins and set aside in a warm place.
4 Finish making the rest of the batter in the same way.
5 To serve, stack up 3-4 pancakes per person, drizzle with Lyle's Golden Syrup and top with a dollop of crème fraîche. Delicious served with fruit salad.

- Or you can make your own pancake mix with 150 g plain flour, 1 teaspoon bicarbonate of soda, pinch salt, 55 g caster sugar, 1 beaten egg, 200 ml milk and a squeeze of lemon juice.

RECIPE COURTESY TATE & LYLE

My Dad

My parents divorced when I was 11, and it was agreed I was old enough to be given the choice of who I wanted to live with and I chose to stay with Dad.

One of our special treats was to go to the pictures once a week to the small cinema in Havant. Dad would also take me to a little café, usually a Friday treat, for plaice and chips or steak and kidney pudding, mash and peas. Lovely!

On my wedding day in 1975, what a sight we must have looked – me in full bridal dress and veil, Dad in his posh suit, taking a drive along Portsmouth sea front in a blue Hillman Imp!

What a special day – Dad doing his proud father bit, and it felt so good to be standing next to him.

Lynda Crossland, Portsmouth, Hants

Above: Lynda and her Dad, Ron, on her wedding day on November 1, 1975
Right: Lynda at her second wedding day, in February last year, but sadly no dad

Joan and David on that memorable evening in 1980

Dear Diary September 19, 1980

Saw him at last, after 35 years of trying to get concert tickets, we actually got to see Sinatra live. He was wonderful, of course!

Got to speak to him, too, and his eyes really are blue. At the end of his performance we rushed up to the front of the stage, and he was about to leave when he noticed us. He came back and shook my hand and said, 'Glad you could make it, ma'am'. He looked straight into my eyes, and six thousand people disappeared. He then took my husband's hand and greeted him warmly, too. Then left the stage.

I'd had the tickets for six months, guarding them with my life – and it took our last £200 but it was worth every penny.

Joan and David Bebbington, Crewe, Cheshire

Meet my pet

I thought this photograph of two of my six cats might make readers laugh!

Marge Wright, Bishops Stortford

I know ladies have to queue for the loo but this beats all!

Top of the hit parade!

5 Nov 1954:
Vera Lynn
My Son My Son

9 Nov 1961:
Elvis Presley
His Latest Flame

6 Nov 1968:
Joe Cocker
With A Little Help
From My Friends

Healthy herbs
Yarrow

A hardy perennial, yarrow is the wild relative of many popular garden varieties. It has small pink-tinged white flowers on upright stems reaching 90cm in height. It can be invasive so keep a watchful eye on it – or pick leaves from plants growing in the wild. The leaves add a piquancy to salads. Botanical name – *Achillea millefolium*

■ **Tip:** Plant yarrow near sickly plants and its root exudates may help the nearby plants recover by boosting their disease resistance.

Recipe of the week

Chunky Chilli Pasta Bake

(Serves 4)

- 450 g (approx 1 lb) beef mince
- 1 onion, peeled and finely chopped
- 2 celery sticks, finely chopped
- 1 small red chilli, deseeded and finely chopped
- 200 g (7 oz) dried pasta shapes, eg penne, fusilli or eliche
- 150 g (5 oz) chestnut mushrooms, cleaned and sliced
- 2 large sprigs fresh thyme leaves, roughly chopped
- 30 ml (2 tablespoons) Madeira wine or sweet sherry
- Salt and freshly milled black pepper
- 500 ml (18 fl oz) good, hot prepared beef gravy
- 50 g (2 oz) grated Mozzarella cheese
- 25 g (1 oz) grated Parmesan
- 30 ml (2 tablespoons) freshly chopped flat-leaf parsley, to garnish

1 Preheat the oven to 190°C, 375°F, Gas Mark 5.
2 Heat a large shallow non-stick frying pan until hot and cook the mince, onion, celery and chilli for 5-7 minutes until brown.
3 Meanwhile, cook the pasta according to the packet instructions, drain and set aside.
4 Add the mushrooms, thyme, Madeira or sherry and seasoning to the mince. Cover, reduce the heat and cook for a further 10 minutes. Stir in the gravy. Mix the cheeses together.
5 Combine the mince and pasta with half the cheese.
6 Spoon the mixture into a 2 litre (3½ pint) ovenproof dish or 4 individual ovenproof dishes. Sprinkle over the remaining cheese and bake for 15-20 minutes.
7 Garnish with freshly chopped parsley before serving with warm crusty bread and a crisp green salad.

RECIPE COURTESY QUALITY STANDARD BEEF

Well I never...

Fear of Hallowe'en is called samhainophobia.

My Dad

Fred with the clock presented to him for his long service to Ealing Hospital

My Father, Frederick, or Fred as he was known, attended Ealing Hospital in the early morning before opening his shop. He was a hairdresser and gave patients a shave.

The testimonial which he received in gratitude for his long service, (and which was also signed by the hospital's Patron HRH Duchess of Kent, as 'Marina') explains it well:

Here is an extract:

King Edward Memorial Hospital, Ealing, W13
'The Committee of Management would like to place on record their great appreciation of the most valuable service which you, Mr Hardy, have rendered to the Hospital over a period of 43 years…
… you have unfailingly carried out your duty to the Hospital patients; that in all weathers and under all conditions, including the very trying war years, you never failed to come to the Hospital and to bring comfort and a cheerful word to the patients'.

Marjorie Day, Seaford, Sussex

Top Tip

Instead of running off the cold water from the hot tap down the drain, save it in a container for washing vegetables and rinsing down.

J Smith, Beaconsfield

Well I never…

'Do you know what I think when I see a pretty girl? …Oh, to be 80 again'.

Louis Calhern in The Magnificent Yankee

Recipe of the week

Fragrant Rice Dessert

- 75 g (3 oz) pudding rice
- 300 ml (½ pint) single cream
- 600 ml (1 pint) whole milk
- 75 g (3 oz) Billington's Unrefined Golden Caster sugar
- Crushed seeds from 4 cardamom pods
- 2 dessertspoons rosewater
- Ground cinnamon or pistachio nuts to decorate

1 Place the rice and cream with almost all the milk in a pan over a low heat.
2 Bring to the boil and then reduce the heat and simmer, uncovered, for 30-40 minutes, stirring from time to time to prevent the rice sticking to the pan, until the rice is tender and the milk is almost absorbed. Add more milk if necessary.
3 Stir in the sugar, cardamom and rosewater and continue cooking until thick and creamy. Pour into serving dishes and leave to cool and set. Sprinkle with cinnamon or pistachios just before serving.

RECIPE COURTESY BILLINGTON'S

Healthy herbs

Juniper

Conifers often receive a bad press, but they're coming back into fashion. Germination is tricky from seed and, being woody they're slow-growing, so it's easier to buy plants from garden centres. You may not traditionally think of juniper as a herb but it can be used medicinally and the berries, which are only produced by female plants, are spicy and can be used when marinading meats. Botanical name – *Juniperus communis*
■**Tip:** Take care when handling as the leaves can irritate.

Top Tip

Make a note of family/ friends' clothes, ring and shoe sizes, so that you can get the right sizes when shopping without them (eg for presents).

My Dad

The one memory of my Dad that stands out was the day I sat in the front seat of the big hall and looked at the platform where the rows of young men were lined up, ordinands for the Methodist Ministry. At least, they were all young except one – my father!

At the age of 61 he was being ordained as a fully-fledged reverend, stepping out into a new phase of his life when others were reaching for their armchair and slippers. Not only was this a wonderful achievement, but for my father it was the fulfilment of a dream.

When he was in his late teens, he felt a call to go into the ministry but there was no money available for his training. This was during the Depression, so he became a brush salesman, and then an office job led to a long career in local government.

Marriage and a family meant there was still no money to spare, but he gave himself unstintingly to the life of the church, as a local preacher, Sunday School superintendent, youth club leader, and choirmaster and organist.

Still the desire remained until that day when it all came true. At that moment I was so proud of him because he had never let go of that dream.

Joyce Halsall, Watchet, Somerset

Joyce's father, Rev Stephen Watts, with his granddaughter, Debbie

That special song

In the late 1950s I went in for a competition in The Daily Mirror to try and win tickets to The Stars At The Palladium. I had to write about the song or singer that had made a difference to my life.

I put pen to paper and said that when I was in a bad mood, or cross about something I would play Joan Regan's May You Always. Her lovely singing of that lovely song would always calm me down and make me feel better.

Well, I won two tickets and took my Mum – and she loved it. It was such a treat for us both and a great night. (I remember Dickie Valentine was on as well.)

Janet Henderson, Chertsey, Surrey

Janet and her mum in the 1950s

Top of the hit parade!

14 Nov 1963:
Gerry & The Pacemakers
You'll Never Walk Alone

17 Nov 1966:
The Beach Boys
Good Vibrations

Meet my pet

My son Edward has always been raised to love animals, so it wasn't a surprise when he wanted his own dog. As he was only nine, he had to save his allowance and do odd jobs to earn the money.

We looked at some lovely Jack Russell terrier pups but as soon as Edward heard that the little tan and white pup suffered fits, he decided he wanted him because he might not get a home.

He named him Stanley and the two of them are devoted to each other. Stanley sits on Edward's shoulders and when he's doing his homework, sleeps on his bed and waits by the door for him every afternoon at school home time.

Stanley's a very brainy little dog and once alerted me when Edward was choking on a sandwich. But he has his daft side too – he loves grapes and I have to buy him a small bunch every Thursday – and when I change the beds, he runs off with the sheets and drags them downstairs!

Despite the fits, Stanley is a wonderful little dog, now five years old but still a puppy at heart.

Kaye Wozencroft, Mitcheldean, Glos

Stanley in a rare quiet moment

Top Tip

Fill bottles with hot water and leave them for a few minutes to help peel labels off.
Shirley Read, Marlow

Well I never...

The budgerigar was introduced into Europe in the 1840s.

Top of the hit parade!

25 Nov 1955:
Bill Haley & His Comets
Rock Around The Clock

19 Nov 1964:
The Supremes
Baby Love

25 Nov 1965:
The Seekers
The Carnival Is Over

Healthy herbs
Lady's Mantle

One plant that everyone should grow in their garden is Lady's Mantle – its pretty leaves look magical when covered in dew and the airy lime-green flowers are a delight. It self-seeds like crazy but, by appearing where it wants, it immediately creates a naturalistic feel to any planting scheme. It thrives in sun or partial shade and all but the wettest soils. Use the young leaves in cooking or add to salads.
Botanical name – *Alchemilla mollis*
■ **Tip:** If you harvest the leaves before flowering you can use them to make a green dye.

Recipe of the week
Latino Beef
(Serves 3 – 4)

- 450g (approx 1 lb) lean beef braising steak cut into chunky cubes
- 5 ml (1 teaspoon) oil
- 2 cloves garlic, crushed
- 25 g (1 oz) chorizo sausage, thinly sliced
- 1 green chilli, cut in half and deseeded
- 30 ml (2 tablespoons) tomato purée
- 8 green olives
- 150 ml (¼ pt) beef stock
- 400 g (approx 1 lb) can chopped tomatoes

1 Heat the oil in a large ovenproof dish. Add the cubed braising steak, and brown all over.
2 Add the crushed garlic, sliced sausage, green chilli, tomato purée, olives, beef stock and can of tomatoes, stir well, cover with a lid and cook for 1½-2 hours at 180°C, 350°F, Gas Mark 4, until meat is tender.
3 Serve with black eye beans and rice, and a fruity salsa of mango and pineapple

RECIPE COURTESY BRITISH MEAT

My Dad

When I was born my mother rejected me – she'd set her heart on a boy and got a bald scrawny five pound girl instead. My father said he was glad, as a girl would not ever have to fight as a soldier, as he had done. He had fought in both battles of The Somme, and had been awarded the Oak Leaf cluster for bravery. (When I came home on leave in 1942, in my khaki ATS uniform, he cried, for he never expected to see his daughter as a soldier.)

Dad was my handsome hero and I adored him. As an only child, my first memories were his teaching me my prayers at night and singing me to sleep with his lovely Welsh voice.

Later on he taught me my times tables, how to ride my fairy bike, to swim and gave me driving lessons in his beloved car, for which he'd scrimped and saved.

He was patience personified, helpful and spoke no ill of anyone. Many years have passed but my children still recall his sense of humour. He adored children and should have had many of his own. I think of him every day and am proud to have been his daughter.

Madeleine J Croll, Whitstable

Left: Madeleine's father, William Henry Rees

Above: Madeleine in her ATS uniform

Recipe of the week

Chocolate Truffle Cake

- 225 g (8 oz) plain chocolate
- 110 g (4 oz) unsalted butter
- 75 ml (3 fl oz) dark rum
- 3 eggs, separated
- 110 g (4 oz) golden caster sugar
- 75 g (3 oz) plain flour
- 75 g (3 oz) ground almonds

For the icing
- 225 g (8 oz) plain chocolate
- 300 ml (10 fl oz) double cream
- 3 teaspoons dark rum
- Cocoa powder

1 Melt chocolate and butter in a bowl over a pan of hot (not boiling) water. Stir in the rum.
2 Place egg yolks and sugar in a bowl over a pan of simmering water and whisk until thick and pale. Remove the bowl from the pan and continue whisking until a trail is left when the whisk is lifted.
3 Stir in the chocolate mixture, ensuring it is blended in evenly. Gently fold in the flour and ground almonds.
4 Whisk the egg whites until stiff and fold into the chocolate mixture, a third at a time until well blended.
5 Pour into a greased, lined 20 cm round cake tin and bake for 45-55 minutes at 180°C, 350°F, Gas Mark 4 until firm in the centre. Turn out and cool on a wire rack.
6 **For the icing:** Melt 110g chocolate with 55 ml cream in a bowl over a pan of hot water. Stir in the rum and leave to cool.
7 Whisk 110 ml cream until thick, add half the rum mixture and mix gently. Cut the cake in half, sandwich together with some of the chocolate icing and spread the remainder over the top and sides.
8 Chill the cake and remaining chocolate rum cream until firm. Melt the rest of the chocolate and cream in a bowl, as before, stir until smooth and allow to cool to lukewarm. Pour over the cake to cover evenly. Shape the chilled chocolate rum mixture into truffles, roll in cocoa powder and arrange on top of the cake.
9 Place in the refrigerator to set.

RECIPE COURTESY BILLINGTON'S

Healthy herbs

Comfrey

Loved by organic gardeners because its leaves make a great fertiliser when infused in water, comfrey is also considered an invasive weed by others. However, whether you're organic or not, it's worth growing to use as a mulch, feed and as a compost accelerator. It has medicinal uses but should only be taken when prescribed by a qualified herbalist. Seeds germination is usually poor so divide plants in autumn or take root cuttings during spring. Botanical name – *Symphytum officinale*

■ **Tip:** Grow the variegated plant as it's more decorative.

Top Tip

After grooming your pet, put the hair in your bird feeder for them to use in their nests.
Sylvia Monk, Sutton-on-Sea

My Dad

One of the proudest moments of my Dad Arthur's life was when he was introduced to Prince Charles, Colonel-in-Chief of the Cheshire Regiment, at the Regiment's Tercentenary re-union in 1989. (Dad volunteered at the age of 16 and it wasn't until he was about to go to the front line that the authorities found out his real age.)

In the photograph, he is telling the Prince how he was in the Guard of Honour when the Prince's great-grandfather, George V, visited the troops in France during the First World War.

Prince Charles asked Dad to what he attributed his good health and long life. With a smile, he said, 'Bacon, egg and lots of fried bread every morning!' I don't think the Prince would have appreciated this as a healthy diet!

Bess Saban, Ellesmere Port, Cheshire

Above: Arthur meeting Prince Charles in 1989

Left: Arthur as a young soldier

Well I never…

Mozart was only five years old when he wrote the melody now sung to Twinkle Twinkle Little Star.

That special song

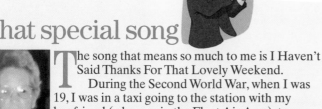

The song that means so much to me is I Haven't Said Thanks For That Lovely Weekend.

During the Second World War, when I was 19, I was in a taxi going to the station with my boyfriend (who was in the Fleet Air Arm), to see him off as he was going back to the Aircraft Carrier on which his plane was based.

We were held up by a traffic jam, and suddenly we heard someone singing this song, which seemed to express everything we felt.

Sadly, the romance didn't last, but we remained friends; even sadder that he became one of the many with 'no known grave', having been shot down over one of Norway's many fjords.

Mrs Clara Skinner, Romsey, Hants

Top of the hit parade!

1 Dec 1966:
Tom Jones
Green-Green Grass Of Home

28 Nov 1970:
Dave Edmonds
I Hear You Knockin'

PIC REPRODUCED BY KIND PERMISSION OF THE EARL OF

On location at Wilton House

Built on holy ground

Wilton House near Salisbury has frequently proved itself to be the perfect setting for period dramas such as the film Mrs Brown, starring Judi Dench and Billy Connolly, and Jane Austen's Sense and Sensibility.

The history of the house stretches back into the mists of time; the present building stands on the site of a ninth century nunnery, founded by King Alfred, which was replaced in the twelfth century by a Benedictine monastery. At the dissolution of the monasteries, Henry VIII gave the land to William Herbert and Wilton House, the home of the present Earl of Pembroke, has remained in the family ever since.

After a fire damaged the building in 1647, seven of the state rooms in the south wing were redesigned by the architects Inigo Jones and John Webb. The most splendid of these is the Double Cube Room which is precisely 30 feet wide, 30 feet high and 60 feet long. The white-painted pine wall is decorated with great swags of foliage and fruit in gold leaf while the gilt and red velvet furniture complements the collection of paintings by Van Dyck.

The front hall of Wilton is dominated by a large statue of William Shakespeare who is said to have produced one of his plays in the house's courtyard.

Wilton is renowned for its gardens. The Palladian Bridge over the River Nadder has always been much admired and copies of it can be seen in other grand settings such as Stowe in Buckinghamshire and Prior Bark, Bath. Other features of the garden include a temple, an orangery, a loggia and an Egyptian column. At the end of the last century, the 17th Earl had a garden created around a fountain in the entrance forecourt in memory of his father.

■ *For further information, phone 01722 746700 or visit the website www.wiltonhouse.co.uk*

Remember when…
Hands, knees, bumps-a-daisy

Albert Tredgett of Enfield had a surprise encounter in the dark

From the 'twopenny rush' as a child to sitting in the one-and-nines as a youth, I was a regular picturegoer.

There were many cinemas in my part of East London from the most palatial to small, rather run-down independent ones. The programmes were usually double features with a change every Monday, Thursday and Sunday. Every cinema might show as many as six films a week and, if I could manage it, I would try to see every one. The trailers were so good, you just had to see the forthcoming film!

The seats were from one shilling for the front stalls to two shillings and three pence for a seat in the circle. I invariably sat in the one-and-nines. When I was single, the shilling seats suited me but when you were courting you were expected to offer a girl a reasonable seat – at the back of the stalls, if possible.

The large cinemas were beautifully furnished with deep pile carpets and upholstered seats. They usually featured an organ recital in the interval.

Even the smaller cinemas were quite comfortable, though not always up to standard. I once went to one of these and the seat in front of me was missing. I didn't mind as it gave me room to stretch my legs. I was immersed in the film when a lady came along the

Albert recalls cinema going at its best

row in front. She was feeling her way along to find a vacant seat and, in doing so, she touched my knees. I don't know who was most shocked, her or me, but she beat a hurried retreat!

We still see the old films repeated again on TV but the experience cannot match that of the good old days at the pictures.

Do I have to eat it?

John Phillpott's memories of school dinners leave a bit of nasty taste…

This wasn't so much a smell, more like an invisible mist that hung in the air. It was a case of mutton meets spotted dick, encounters grey cabbage on the way, and then combines with jam roly-poly… yes, school dinners left an indelible mark on my memory.

Or, perhaps, we should say tastebuds. Well, no we couldn't, actually – for the defining characteristics of school grub in the 1950s was that it was tasteless.

I attended a village school, which meant that the daily rations had to be transported at least four miles in steel containers.

These may have kept the contents hot, but that was about all. For when this overcooked sludge was eventually extricated, the meat had the texture of cardboard and anything called 'greens' was certainly someone's idea of a joke.

The consumption of this sludge was compulsory. Headmistress Mrs James made sure it was. I was very, very afraid of Mrs James. However, she was at her sternest when it came to school dinners. You had to eat every scrap.

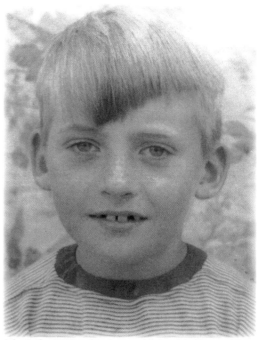

John in the 1950s – dripping wouldn't melt in his mouth!

One day, I was told to take my plate of unfinished food to afternoon lessons. It had been made quite clear to me that I would not be leaving school that day until all the rapidly congealing fragments of semolina pudding had been consumed.

"Think of all those starving children in Abyssinia, John Phillpott!" boomed Mrs James. The meal I most dreaded was salad. I knew, even then, that green vegetables were good for you, but I always objected to the inclusion of live protein that could often be found lurking under a lettuce leaf.

I'm not sure whether the consumption of the occasional earthworm came under the semolina pudding rule but, maybe, time has erased such traumas from my memory. Suffice to say that it was this, coupled with the arterial stain left by beetroot on mashed spuds, that made me long for the next day when the food would at least be hot.

In those days, the midday meal was called 'dinner' and in the evening it was 'tea'. This was always a far more appetising prospect, mainly because it was not only recognisable as being edible, but also freshly made.

There was a fixed cycle to the week. On Monday, mother always served egg and chips, this being a simple dish for a washday. On Tuesdays, it was invariably herrings, as this was the earliest that fresh fish could reach the Midlands.

Wednesday was mixed grill, then on Thursdays and Fridays, it would be cheese or sardines on toast. Saturday was salad day – it didn't matter whether it was spring, summer, autumn or winter.

Many a Sunday winter's tea time was spent around the fire. Southerners call them crumpets, but in the Midlands and North they were known as pikelets. These were suspended over hot coals with toasting forks and then plastered with butter and Bovril.

However, the best treat was the dripping from that day's roast. Buckets of beef fat would be ladled on to toast and then covered in salt.

Leaving food was universally frowned on, too – many a child of that long-lost decade after the war was informed in no uncertain manner that there would be no 'afters' if the first course wasn't all eaten.

Nowadays, making children finish their meals is mainly frowned upon. But youngsters in the 1950s enjoyed a far more varied diet than their modern counterparts, one that created the strong constitutions needed in adulthood.

So, if Mrs James is out there somewhere, I'd like to thank her. It may have been awful at the time, but she taught me some table manners. And, come to think of it, the semolina pudding wasn't that bad, either.

Decision Time

by Joan Killen

The problem arises every year – where to go for Christmas?

It was a frosty night in early December. Judith inched nearer to the gas fire as she drank her cocoa.

"What are we going to do for Christmas, then?" asked Graham.

Judith sighed: "I'm not sure."

"Well, we must make our minds up soon, otherwise it's not fair on the children."

Their son, Paul, was 32 and daughter, Maggie, 27. The problem for their parents was having to choose between two separate family invitations for Christmas.

"Last year Paul and Chloe went skiing and Maggie and the boys came to us so really it's Paul and Chloe's turn."

Graham and Judith were proud of their son, Paul. He had always been an industrious boy and was now a successful accountant. Responsible and thoughtful, he never forgot a birthday or anniversary. Chloe was the ideal wife for him and they were both high fliers.

Judith was fond of them both, but sometimes felt a little over-awed by their success. They had highly paid jobs and their house in Bath was decorated to perfection. When Judith and Graham had visited the couple over Easter, they were stunned by the creamy walls,

honey-coloured wood floors and antique furniture. Their en-suite bathroom was tiled in white and Judith had been a little nervous of the power shower.

"I know that we should go to Bath," she said, "but to be honest I just don't feel completely at home there. It's all so perfect and, if Chloe asks neighbours in for drinks, I'll feel out of my depth."

Graham agreed. "I know what you mean, so shall we ask Maggie and the grandchildren here then?"

Judith replied: "No, she wants us to go to her for Christmas Day."

"But she hasn't even got a big enough table!" Graham exclaimed.

Maggie often wondered how they had produced two such different offspring. While Paul had never been any trouble, Maggie was always high-spirited and, as an adolescent, a real rebel.

Judith recalled the confrontations over late nights, unsuitable friends and loud music. Aged 17, Maggie had run off with a divorced man. A year later she was back home, pregnant and deserted. She had to grow up very quickly when she had twin boys.

Judith and Graham rallied round and Maggie moved into

a council house. They had to admit that she had provided a happy home for the boys. Now that Ben and James were at school, Maggie had a job as a dinner lady. However, the house was in a permanent state of chaos with football boots and school books scattered around.

Graham was right – there was no way that Maggie could produce anything resembling a proper Christmas dinner!

Judith stood and stretched: "I'm going to have a soak in the bath. Let's make a decision; you ring Paul and accept for Christmas, then I'll ring Maggie later."

Relaxing in the lavender-scented water, Judith let her imagination roam. If they had the money how wonderful it would be to take the family away. She pictured a country house hotel with roaring log fires. On Christmas Day they would walk to the village church, returning to a sumptuous meal. Afterwards the children would play snowballs while the adults sipped Champagne and nibbled mince pies.

'Fantasy!' Judith thought as she donned pyjamas and dressing gown. Now to ring Maggie; she hoped her daughter wouldn't be too disappointed that they had decided to go to Bath.

"Did you speak to Paul?" she asked Graham.

If they had the money how wonderful it would be to take the family away

Timsharvle.©om

"Comfortable! It will be like having a holiday in a five-star hotel"

His brow furrowed, he replied: "Yes – Paul and Maggie have decided that as we hadn't accepted either of their invitations for Christmas, we probably wanted a quiet time on our own. So he and Chloe have invited Maggie and the boys down there."

There was an uneasy silence as each pursued their own thoughts. Graham was worried that Judith felt left out of the family celebrations while Judith tried to picture their two boisterous grandsons in Paul's perfect house.

Striding to the phone, she dialled Maggie's number.

"Mum, great, I was going to ring you tonight."

Judith took a deep breath. "I just wanted to talk about Christmas," she started.

"It's going to be wonderful –

we're going down to Paul's – he's treating us to the train fare."

"Do you think you will be…" Judith hesitated, "er, comfortable there?"

"Comfortable! It will be like having a holiday in a five-star hotel."

"What about the boys?" Judith ventured.

"There's a room they haven't decorated yet. They'll have camp beds and a portable TV. It's right at the top of the house so they can make as much noise as they like. Could I have a quick word with Dad?"

Dazed, Judith handed the phone to Graham.

It was a strange feeling – a Christmas on their own for the first time since they were

newly married.

"Well, just us old folks then," she said as Graham came back into the room.

He gave a small grimace: "Not quite – she couldn't find anyone to look after Moses, so we have a guest for Christmas."

"Not that great lolloping dog!"

They looked at each other in stunned silence, then Graham said: "Look on the bright side, he can eat all the leftovers."

"We can take him for long walks and get some of the extra pounds off," added Judith.

They started to laugh; after thirty-five years of family life they were used to making adjustments. Next year they would plan ahead with no room for silly misunderstandings.

Saturday

1

Sunday

2

Advent Sunday

Monday

3

Tuesday

4

Wednesday

5

Thursday

6

Friday

7

Saturday

8

Sunday

9

Monday

10

Tuesday

11

Wednesday

12

Thursday

13

Friday

14

Saturday

15

Sunday

16

Monday

17

Tuesday

18

Wednesday

19

Thursday

20

Friday

21

Saturday

22

Winter Solstice

Sunday **23**	Friday **28**
Monday **24**	Saturday **29**
Tuesday **25** Christmas Day	Sunday **30**
Wednesday **26** Boxing Day	Monday **31** New Year's Eve
Thursday **27**	

By the fireside

Dancing flames, flickering bright,
Cosy and warm, lighting the night.
Purring, content, the cat's on my lap,
Ready for his evening nap.

Slippered feet, red wine at hand,
By the fireside, I'm feeling grand.
Twinkling stars in the night sky,
Cold whistling wind, whipping by.

Be content with simple things,
And see what pleasure your life brings.

Susan Bean, Epsom Downs, Surrey

PIC: GARY GEROVAC/MASTERFILE

Top of the hit parade!

6 Dec 1967:
The Beatles
Hello Goodbye

7 Dec 1974:
Barry White
You're The First, The Last,
My Everything

My Dad

I only knew my Dad, George, for 11 years, but what a wealth of memories I have of him. His patience, for one thing. He was a keen gardener and had been planning rows of potatoes, only to find when he'd finished, that his 'helpful' daughter had been behind him, taking the potatoes out of their holes.

During the war years he'd been sent home on what was called 'survivors' leave. His ship had been torpedoed and so he came to school to bring my sister and I home. Suddenly, he caught us up and tossed us over a garden hedge, laying over us as we were machine-gunned by enemy aircraft. Scary but we were safe with Dad.

He was killed in 1942 in the Arctic Convoys choosing, when the order was given to abandon ship, to stay with the wounded, handing round cigarettes and chocolate, rather than save himself. By his example, I am able to live my life today and I remember with pride those precious years with my wonderful Dad.
Terry Yeoman, Swansea

Terry's dad, George Albert Drummond

Well I never...

The average price of a Christmas card is 71p.

Healthy herbs
Hop

An essential ingredient in the brewing industry, the hop first became important during Tudor times. A hardy herbaceous perennial that climbs, a hop plant can easily reach 9m in height. It enjoys a sunny position and a soil rich in organic matter. Pick the young shoots during spring, steam them and add to salads.
Botanical name – *Humulus lupulus*
■ **Tip:** Buy the golden hop *Humulus lupulus* 'Aureus' because it's far prettier.

Recipe of the week

Zesty Syrup Pud
(Serves 2)

- 50 g (2 oz) butter, plus extra for greasing
- 3 tablespoons Lyle's Golden Syrup
- ½ lemon, zest and juice
- 1 rounded tablespoon plain flour, plus extra for dusting
- 1 egg yolk
- 1 egg
- 2 tablespoons caster sugar
- Lyle's Golden Syrup to serve

1 Grease 2 ramekins or heatproof coffee cups with some butter and dust with some plain flour. This will prevent sticking. Melt the butter, Lyle's Golden Syrup and lemon zest and juice together and leave to cool.
2 Whisk the yolk, whole egg and sugar until pale and light, then gently fold in the flour and the syrup mixture. Divide the mixture between the ramekins and cook in the microwave for 2-4 minutes or until they've set. Alternatively, cook in the oven at 200°C, 400°F, Gas Mark 6 for 8-10 minutes.
3 Pour Lyle's Golden Syrup over the top and serve immediately with a scoop of vanilla ice cream.

RECIPE COURTESY TATE & LYLE

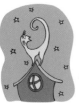

Meet my pet

Our pet cat, Tiger, is not a cuddlesome cat. He's 13 years old and mad! I have to tell people not to stroke him, as he has a habit of trying to attack ladies' legs, and has done this ever since he was a kitten.

Our friend, when she writes, always asks about our 'mad cat' but we still love him, even though he sometimes looks longingly at my legs!

Mrs S Sellers, Newark

Watch out, there's a tiger on the prowl…

Your December health

The festive season may be fun, but it can play havoc with your sleep patterns. If you're finding it hard to nod off, eat foods high in the amino acid tryptophan, which can help promote sleep. Bananas, dates and – luckily – turkey are all good sources. Sprinkle a few drops of sedative lavender essential oil on your pillow before bed, and tuck yourself up with a mug of soothing camomile tea.

Recipe of the week

Chunky Pork Chops with Sage, Garlic & Lemon

(Serves 4)

- 4 lean, thick pork chops
- 3 cloves garlic
- Black pepper
- 6 fresh sage leaves, roughly chopped
- Juice and rind of one lemon
- 30 ml (2 tablespoons) olive oil

For the butter

- 50 g (2 oz) butter
- Juice and rind of ½ lemon
- 30 ml (2 tablespoons) Parmesan cheese, grated
- 5 fresh sage leves
- Baby veg for dipping

1 Crush together (either using a pestle & mortar or bowl and wooden spoon) the garlic, black pepper and sage leaves. Add to this lemon juice and rind and olive oil.

2 Place the pork chops in a large bowl and add the marinade mixture, smear all over the chops, cover and refrigerate for about 2 hours.

3 **Buttery dip**: Add to a small bowl the butter, lemon juice and rind, Parmesan cheese and sage leaves. Place in the microwave for about 1 minute, or until melted. Stir together.

4 Cook chops on a preheated grill, griddle or barbecue for 6-8 minutes per side.

5 Serve with a selection of baby seasonal vegetables eg sugar snap peas, asparagus, baby sweetcorn, baby carrots, baby fennel for dipping – raw or plunged into boiling water, plus a wedge of crusty bread

RECIPE COURTESY BRITISH MEAT

Healthy herbs

Pot marigold

Pretty as a picture, the pot marigold is a popular herb. It's simply grown from seed sown in spring and will brighten the garden all summer with its sunshine yellow flowers. Plant in a sunny position in well-drained soil and deadhead regularly to encourage more flowers. Use the young flowers and leaves in salads.

Botanical name – *Calendula officinalis*

■ **Tip:** Plant a few in a colourful container and use as a table centre in the garden.

Top Tip

To dispose of personal details on documents, soak in boiling water and washing up liquid and it will disintegrate.

I Aston, Hednesford

Well I never…

The Queen and the Duke of Edinburgh send more than 800 Christmas cards a year.

My Dad

When I was young, I was my father's constant companion, always listening to his stories, especially those of his time in France during the First World War. He only told me nice things about the people he met, or about the farm in Normandy where he spent some time.

He'd left school very young and a good education for us was his top priority. When I went to Grammar School I was soon showing off with my newly acquired French. One evening at the supper table, he surprised us all by pointing at the bread – 'du pain', then the butter 'du buerre'. Gaining confidence, he pointed at the mustard, 'passez moo de la'.

It's 'moi' not 'moo' I corrected. He'd probably never seen it written down, but learned by listening. He didn't say anything, just smiled.

Later, on my first trip to France with the school, I addressed the hotel staff in my exaggerated accent. They laughed at me and replied in English. I remembered then how my Dad had survived for four years with his 'trench French' – I hadn't lasted four minutes with mine.

Jean White, Sunbury on Thames, Middx

Top: Jean, daughter Victoria and father Thomas in 1966
Above: Jean, daughter Amanda and granddaughter Olivia in 2005

Top of the hit parade!

16 Dec 1955:
Dickie Valentine
Christmas Alphabet

13 Dec 1962:
Elvis Presley
Return To Sender

3 Dec 1964:
Rolling Stones
Little Red Rooster

That special song

'I love you, what more can I say,
Believe me, there's no other way,
I love you, I will to the end,
There, I've said it again'

In August 1945 my parents and I were invited to a welcome home party held for the local boys returning back after serving four years abroad with the eighth army.

Alfie, my husband-to-be, was the youngest of the group. He was 24 and I was 18 and it was love at first sight, and when we were married six months later, they said it wouldn't last.

My first present from him was a record of Issy Bonn singing, There, I've Said It Again and Alfie said, 'It's to tell you all the things I find difficult to say. It remained our song for our lifetime together. We celebrated our Golden Wedding in 1996 and sadly my husband died just after his 80th birthday.

Over the years my record was lost, and no one seemed to remember Issy Bonn or our song, but… last year I went into a shop to buy a CD with my daughter, and smiling from the front of a CD was Issy Bonn and the fifth track was our song. It was like a message from Alfie all over again.

Maureen Best, Wootton Bassett, Wilts

Above: Maureen and Alfie's wedding day in 1946
Left: Maureen and Alfie in 2001

My Dad

My Dad, Cliff Shepherd, is 92 and in 2005, completed 60 years of being Assistant Father Christmas at our village Rainbows Christmas parties.

He first started when he came home from the war and has done it without a break at Sunday School, play groups, mother and toddler groups and Brownies. My mum is in a local residential home and he escorts Matron on her rounds on Christmas morning and gives presents to the residents.

He's a wonderful Dad.

Thelma Handford, Stamford, Lincs

Father Christmas (Cliff) handing out presents

Healthy herbs
Perilla

It may be fairly new on the gardening scene in this country but perilla is a great bedding plant. A hardy annual, it can easily reach 90cm in height and has vibrant purple leaves with crinkled edges – these are extremely aromatic when crushed. Sow seed in spring and grow in sun or partial shade. Pick the leaves and use them fresh in stir-fries or as a dye when pickling. If you're brave enough to try sushi, then use the flowerheads as a seasoning. Botanical name – *Perilla frutescens purpurascens*

■ **Tip:** Use its coloured leaves throughout your borders to create contrast.

Meet my pet

This is George, my 12-year-old Cocker Spaniel. I've had him since he was 10 months old and abandoned at Wood Green Animal Sanctuary.

After a good walk, he really enjoys his sleep!

Julia Garratt, Peterborough

George just dropping off

Top of the hit parade!

20 Dec 1969:
Rolf Harris
Two Little Boys

23 Dec 1972:
Jimmy Osmond
Long Haired Lover From Liverpool

21 Dec 1974:
Mud
Lonely This Christmas

Recipe of the week

Ivy and husband, Ronald, enjoying their cruise, Christmas 1965

Dear Diary

August 1965

I have always kept a diary and for me the year 1965 was the most memorable. We were on holiday at Newquay with two friends, sitting on the cliff top, reading the Sunday paper, when suddenly my friend said, 'Look, your name's in the paper. You've won a cruise on the Queen Mary this Christmas'.

It was the experience of a lifetime which I will never forget. We left Southampton on December 23 and sailed to Las Palmas. We had many famous names to entertain us – Jessie Matthews, Max Wall, Max Jaffa, The Applejacks, Norman Wisdom – and Jimmy Tarbuck was at Waterloo to wish us 'bon voyage'. It was floating luxury, with all the trimmings.

Mrs Ivy Weston, Bognor Regis

Christmas Tree Decorations
(Makes 12)

- 25 g (1 oz) Fruisana Fruit Sugar
- 25 g (1 oz) butter
- 1 tablespoon black treacle
- 2 tablespoons golden syrup
- 150 g (5 oz) plain flour
- ½ teaspoon baking powder
- ½ teaspoon ground ginger
- Icing sugar, colourings, Christmas themed cutters to decorate

1 Preheat oven to 180°C, 350°F, Gas Mark 4. Melt the butter, Fruisana, treacle and syrup. Leave to cool.
2 Sift the flour, baking powder and ginger in a bowl and stir into the melted mixture to make a dough.
3 Roll out to a thickness of 5 mm (¼ inch) and cut out using a Christmas themed cutter. Place on greased baking trays and bake for 10 minutes.
4 When cool, use coloured icing and decorative balls to decorate.

RECIPE COURTESY FRUISANA

Well I never...

'We are having the same old things for Christmas dinner this year... relatives'.

Mark Twain

Top Tip

Paint your house number with fluorescent paint so it can be quickly recognised by the emergency services.

Charlotte Primrose, Lawford

Recipe of the week
Cranberry Glazed Beef with Mulled Wine Gravy

- Lean beef sirloin joint
- 8-10 shallots, peeled

For the glaze
- 45 ml (3 tablespoons) cranberry sauce
- 45 ml (3 tablespoons) mulled wine

For the gravy
- 300 ml (½ pt) beef stock
- 150 ml (¼ pt) mulled wine
- 30 ml (2 tablespoons) cranberry sauce
- 15 ml (1 tablespoons) gravy granules

Open-roast the beef at 180°C, 350°F, Gas Mark 4 for the calculated cooking time*. 50 minutes before the end add the shallots to the roasting tin.

For the glaze
Mix the 3 tablespoons of cranberry sauce with 3 tablespoons of mulled wine. Brush over the beef during the last 15 minutes of cooking time. Once cooked, wrap the beef in foil.

To make the gravy
Add the hot beef stock to the roasting tin and stir to mix with any meat juices. Drain off any excess fat and transfer to a saucepan. Add the remaining mulled wine and cranberry sauce. Bring to the boil for 5-10 minutes, add the gravy granules and stir until thickened.

- *Cooking times*
Rare – 20 minutes per 450g (1 lb) plus 20 minutes
Medium – 25 minutes per 450g (1 lb) plus 25 minutes
Well done – 30 minutes per 450g (1 lb) plus 30 minutes

RECIPE COURTESY BRITISH MEAT

Well I never...

'The Queen's Christmas speech was first televised in 1957'.

Dear Diary
December 25, 2005

Outside Christmas lights not working. I don't know a thing about electrics. Gave each bulb a small twist, nothing happened, so thought I'd look at the plug. Felt very pleased when I changed the fuse and the lights worked.

Accidentally poured hot jelly over my hand when making a trifle for tea, luckily the scald spray was close by. It hurt a lot between my fingers, but did not want to alarm my stroke victim husband, so carried on and made custard without further mishap.

4pm: The outside light refuses to work. I went up into the loft with a torch tucked under my chin, removing the cover on the fuse box. From my large collection of fuses – well, they were my husband's but they're mine now – I replaced it, and the light worked, and when my love smiled and nodded, I knew I had done it right.

I'm waiting for the day when a tile slips and I have to go up on the roof – and I'm 75 in two days time.
Eileen Neuman, Trainee Electrician of Bolsover, Derbys

Top of the hit parade!

29 Dec 1960:
Cliff Richard
I Love You

28 Dec 1961:
Danny Williams
Moon River

Healthy herbs

Olive

Climate change has enabled more of us to grow less hardy plants in our gardens. Olives can now be grown outside in sheltered gardens – but unless they receive plenty of sunshine, they're unlikely to produce much fruit. Make sure the soil is well-drained and protect the plants from the winter wet. Cut back the plants during spring and make sure they're fed and watered regularly during summer. You can hardly make olive oil out of the fruit you produce but you can make an antiseptic wash by infusing the leaves in water. Any olives you harvest should be soaked in oil, or they will remain unpalatable. Olives may reach 10m in height but you can buy small bushes or miniature standards from garden centres.

Botanical name – *Olea europea*

■ **Tip:** Olive oil makes a great laxative.

My Dad

All the family was sat around the table when my father said, ' I've just seen a wonderful sight. When I was letting the cows out from milking, Father Christmas, with his reindeer and sleigh went gliding across the sky just above me. It was dusk and the old oil lamp on his sleigh lit it up beautifully'.

Well, my brother and myself were overwhelmed with excitement; we left the table and dashed outside. I will always remember this and have told the story to my grandchildren and great-grandchildren.

Doreen Neal, Warwick

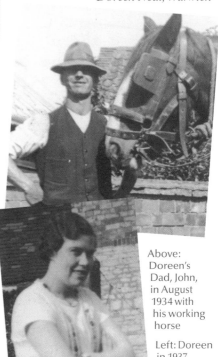

Above: Doreen's Dad, John, in August 1934 with his working horse

Left: Doreen in 1937

That special song

Whenever I hear the carol Silent Night I am transported back more than 78 years, to when I was eight years old.

We were gathered in a wooden classroom at the end of the Christmas term. In the corner stood the tree lit with candles. Stanley, one of the pupils and choirboy at the local church, stood by the tree singing Silent Night so movingly.

Hilda Wells, Fareham, Hants

Top Tip

When undoing a jar lid, put on a pair of rubber gloves to give you extra grip.
Helen Haden, Solihull

PIC: JAMES BRITTAIN

On location at Greenwich

Wren's grand design

Said to be the great baroque masterpiece of English architecture, the Old Royal Naval College at Greenwich has naturally attracted the attention of many production crews. Scenes for the film The Madness of King George were shot here, as well as for the TV production Longitude in which Greenwich had an important historic role to play.

Greenwich Hospital was established in 1694 by Royal Charter for the relief and support of seamen and their dependants and for the improvement of navigation. Sir Christopher Wren, who planned the site, described it as 'one of the most sublime sights English architecture affords'. His grand design was completed by two other eminent architects,

Hawksmoor and Vanbrugh.

The elaborate ceiling and wall paintings in the Great Hall (also known as the Painted Hall) were executed by Sir James Thornhill between 1707 and 1726. The chapel was restored after a fire in 1779.

The seamen, or pensioners, who were housed in Greenwich were given pocket money of one shilling a week. They lived on a diet of bread, beer and boiled meat and smoked their clay pipes in the Chalk Walk, now known as the Skittle Alley. ('Chalk' was another name for a clay pipe.)

In 1873, the complex of

buildings became the Royal Naval College where officers from all over the world came to train in the naval sciences. The Navy moved out in 1998 and today the buildings are home to the University of Greenwich and Trinity College of Music. The College is administered by a charity, the Greenwich Foundation, which arranges a wide variety of activities that include daily guided tours as well as open-air theatre and opera, concerts and exhibitions.

■ *For further information, phone 020 8269 4763 or visit the website www.greenwichfoundation.org.uk*

Remember when...

Matron was awesome

Mrs F A Connolly of Bexhill-on-Sea had to spend Christmas in hospital

In 1948, aged nine, I was in hospital after being knocked down by a van while crossing the road. I remember regaining consciousness in the ambulance and the next thing I recall is coming round on a ward with my leg in plaster, raised in the air on a pulley with weights on the end. I was on an adult ward with one other child, named Victoria.

The ward had ten to 15 beds down each side with French doors at one end leading to a balcony. On nice days, some of the beds would be pushed outside for a change of scenery.

The matron came round every night. She walked very briskly and inspected every patient by

shining her torch on you. She was rather awesome. Every bed had to be neat and tidy for the doctors' round and if you were up in a chair you were not allowed to lie on top of the bed. Visitors could certainly not sit on the bed.

I was in hospital from October to February so I spent Christmas there. We collected sweet papers and asked our visitors to bring silver paper from chocolate bars which we twisted into rosette shapes. The nurses brought twigs and we wired the rosette 'flowers' to them to decorate the ward. A big tree was placed at one end of the ward and on Christmas Eve the doctors and nurses came round singing carols.

Christmas in hospital for this girl

My parents left my presents and they were put on the bottom of the bed for when I woke up. Father Christmas came and gave everyone on the ward a present. Thinking back now, I think how nice it was that we were not forgotten even though we were not on a children's ward.

Christmas trivia

Test your knowledge with these festive teasers – if you get stuck the answers are at the bottom of the page.

PICTUREFEATURES

1 Which of these names does NOT belong to one of Santa's reindeer?
a) Comet
b) Prancer
c) Blitzen
d) Klaxon

2 If you were given frumenty at a Medieval Christmas party, what would you do with it?
a) Eat it
b) Burn it
c) Put it in your hair
d) Use it to polish your boots

3 Which of these names does NOT belong to one of the Three Kings?
a) Caspar
b) Balthazar
c) Teleost
d) Melchior

4 In Tchaikovsky's ballet The Nutcracker, who is the Nutcracker's main enemy?
a) A girl called Clara
b) The King of the Mice
c) Dr Almond
d) Drosselmeyer the magician

5 The poinsettia is a traditional Christmas flower. Where did it originally grow?
a) Canada
b) China
c) Mexico
d) Spain

6 Where did the Christmas tree tradition originate?
a) Germany
b) Israel
c) New England, USA
d) Scandinavia

7 Celebrating Christmas was once against the law in...?
a) Holland
b) Indiana
c) Massachusetts, USA
d) Japan

8 What significance is holly in celebrating Christmas?
a) The pointed leaves represent the Star of Bethlehem
b) It was mistaken for mistletoe
c) The red berries are a Christmas colour
d) The early church banned mistletoe, so holly was substituted

9 In the song, The 12 Days of Christmas, what did my true love give on the fifth day?
a) Pipers piping
b) Lords a-leaping
c) Gold rings
d) Maids milking

10 In the film It's A Wonderful Life (above) how do you know that a new angel has got his wings?
a) A cock crows
b) There is a lightning flash
c) A bell rings
d) A trumpet sounds